The Either/Or Investor

The Either/Or Investor

How to Succeed in Global Investing,
One Decision at a Time

Clark Winter

RANDOM HOUSE NEW YORK

The Either/Or Investor is a commonsense guide to personal finance. In practical advice books, as in life, there are no guarantees, and readers are cautioned to rely on their own judgment about their individual circumstances and to act accordingly.

Copyright © 2008 by Clark Winter

Published in the United States by Random House, an imprint of The Random House Publishing Group, a division of Random House, Inc., New York.

RANDOM HOUSE and colophon are registered trademarks of Random House, Inc.

ISBN 978-1-4000-6592-9

LIBRARY OF CONGRESS CATALOGING-IN-PUBLICATION DATA

Winter, Clark.
The either/or investor : how to succed in global investing, one decision at a time / Clark Winter.
p.   cm.
Includes index.
ISBN 978-1-4000-6592-9
1. Investments.   2. Finance, Personal.   I. Title.
HG4521.W4898 2007
332.6—dc22   2006035798

Printed in the United States of America on acid-free paper

www.atrandom.com

9 8 7 6 5 4 3 2 1

FIRST EDITION

Book design by Simon M. Sullivan

To my wife and family
for their inspiration and support

PREFACE

The Either/Or Investor is a book I have now written three times. The first time, I wrote it in my head as I gave talks to clients in my own money-management business and at Citi Global Wealth Management, where I worked before moving to Goldman Sachs. There are some people who, when they speak, overly complicate matters because they are attempting to impress you with their expertise. I've always been most impressed, though, by those who are able to take really complicated material and make it intelligible to ordinary people, so they can take action on their own and not have to rely upon experts. So as I went around the world speaking with people, I constantly tried to hone my messages.

The second time came when I actually sat down to write *The Either/Or Investor*. I realized that smart people approach problems as dichotomies—either/or decisions. If this, then not that. If yes, if no, then what? It is a sound way to think, and it allowed me to characterize problems in a way that makes sense to investors. But you'll have to be the judge of how successful I've been.

The third time I wrote the book was after it was finished and had been sent off to the publisher. The subprime mortgage crisis exploded, and while the book as I had written it turned out to be remarkably prescient in alluding to the problems of easy credit, I decided that allusions are too indirect, and permit an author to proclaim success too easily in reading the tea leaves. So I have reworked the book and tried to tackle the credit crisis more directly.

When I began writing this work, I organized it to reflect my belief that investors need to remain abreast of a constantly changing world. So must I.

CLARK WINTER

March 2008

CONTENTS

Why We Are Here

My name is Clark Winter. Over several decades, I've worked in the financial services industry, including running my own firm. In my thirty years in the investment industry, I've traded currencies for billionaire hedge fund managers. I've managed portfolios for high-net-worth clients. I've created my own advisory group to help clients find the best investment advice. I'm confident that I have handled almost every financial instrument, from common stock to currency arbitrage, and can explain all of them to ordinary people.

These days I travel the world listening to and talking with clients and executives. I present clients with my synthesis of all the information I read and hear. I don't repeat what other investors are saying. I show investors the facts, and, because investors tend to be smart, curious people, they can generally figure out the investment implications for themselves. Often, in fact, *they* tell *me* how I ought to be investing, and their ideas are often quite sound. Over the years, as I have traveled around, clients, investors, and friends have repeatedly told me that I should write a book about investing, because I do have a way with words and I can explain complicated things simply. Frankly, I had no interest in writing a book about personal finance or investing. There are thousands of books on the subject, and I'm just not vain enough to think that I can add to what they say.

I have a fundamental problem with the personal-finance books on the market: They substitute *wishing and hoping* for *understanding*. They tell readers what other investors have successfully achieved in the past, implying that if readers do the same, they can achieve the same dazzling results. These books do this with a straight face—with no caveat emptor or follow-up proof that the advice actually works. These books sell *aspiration* rather than inspiration, and to me, wishing without the ability to act is not hope, but rather its opposite.

Despite my reservations, I began to believe that I might write a book, but one in which investing was the object rather than the subject. Indeed, the subject of this book is sound decision making. One of the things I've learned in my years in the investment business is that great investing is really about understanding how to evaluate the facts in front of you, how to make reasonable suppositions about the things you don't know, how to account for the uncertainties that impede decision making, and finally, how to do all that rapidly enough so that you can gain an advantage over competitors and thus the market. The purpose of this book is to link the two skill sets, investing and decision making.

One of the earliest things that I discovered about decision making in general is that the smartest executives and the most successful investors have a unique ability to process an enormous amount of information and boil it down into *binaries* that simplify decision making. Yes or no is a binary. Go or stay is a binary. Love or hate is a binary. In investing, the first and most important binary is fear or greed. I could spend hours talking about this, but the basic idea is that in a time of greed, investors dwell somewhere between optimism and irrational exuberance, driving up the price (if not the value) of everything. When fear dominates the collective investing mind, perfectly sound investments tread water or suffer. Fear and greed are imprecise notions, to be sure. But as Justice Potter Stewart said of pornography, you know them when you see them.

This either/or description of circumstances, I've found, resonates with clients, regardless of their financial sophistication. It helps them understand what's going on and why, and it helps them make better decisions.

A friend asked me the other day why his General Electric shares had languished in the high 20s and mid-30s for the last several years—usually less than half of GE's January 2000 high of $72 a share. It didn't make sense. GE was an amazing company. Since the retirement of its legendary

CEO, Jack Welch, the company had answered all concerns about its new CEO, Jeff Immelt, and was firing on all cylinders. It had made major acquisitions and divestitures and had clearly positioned itself to be the infrastructure supplier of choice for the developing world, especially China and India. It had the largest market capitalization of any U.S. company and, even with $170 billion in annual revenues, was growing earnings 15 percent to 19 percent a year. Because the company's price/earnings multiple continued to fall for nearly five years, the company itself thought the share price was a bargain and was instituting a $15 billion stock buyback program.

"This is a great company," he said. "Why doesn't the market see that?"

"It's fear," I told my friend in a capsule version of what I tell clients. Since the collapse of the Internet and telecom bubbles in 2000 and the post-9/11 rise of terrorism, fear has been the prime mover in world equity markets. Investors would rather keep their money in cash than put it to work in stocks. Thus, while markets have come back from their post-2001 lows, they have barely risen past their pre-2000 highs, despite record earnings from many companies and decent performance from many more. Fear drives investors into preservation strategies; greed makes them commit to growth. As long as investors continue to hear bad news, fear will hover over their investing choices—and GE's share price will lag behind the company's actual performance.

I left it to my friend to infer the obvious response: Buy GE. It's a bargain. As fear gives way to optimism (and its sibling, greed), GE's stock should eventually come around. Meanwhile, please pay attention to the issues Jeff Immelt discusses in his work and his written contributions. He's right on target when he highlights the major problems and opportunities the world is facing.

Fear versus greed is just one of the binary couplings I use to assess markets. There are hundreds of them, depending upon how much information you need to make an investment decision, but for practical purposes, just about all investment thinking can be explained with slightly fewer than two dozen binaries, which I will discuss in the pages to come. Some of them deal with the world at large, some deal with investors' thinking, and some deal with how to make investment choices and how to make sure a money manager is making the right decisions for you. Until now, I have been presenting these binaries only to my colleagues and high-net-worth clients. In discussing them here, I hope to rid people of the need to imitate other investors so slavishly *and* to provide them with an understanding of market forces so that they can think for themselves. If people understand, they won't have to be told what to do.

That's me. Now, what about you? You might be someone like my friend Steve, a prosperous investment banker who is also a fanatical golfer. He spends a king's ransom annually on club memberships, golf vacations, lessons, instructional videos, and new equipment. He's the kind of guy who has a putting green set up in his office and practices his golf swing whenever he's on a conference call. As for his golf budget, he spends the money without qualms or any of the usual risk-versus-reward hesitation he would apply to other large expenditures and to the investments he makes or involves his company in. Golf is his passion, and he is determined to whittle his respectable 10 handicap down to single digits—thus demonstrating that golf handicaps and cell phones are the only two things about which men will boast that "mine is smaller." At no point, however, in this massive investment of time, money, and effort does Steve ever imagine that he will be as good as Tiger Woods. He's fanatical, but he's not deluded.

Another friend, John, is a culinary connoisseur. He has a state-of-the-art kitchen in his Connecticut home. He has a priceless wine cellar. He subscribes to a dozen cooking magazines. John's idea of a perfect vacation is two weeks at a cooking school in Italy. As Steve loves to golf, John loves to cook, devoting much of his free time to preparing gourmet meals for his family and friends. At no point, however, does John ever imagine opening up a restaurant and becoming Jean-Georges Vongerichten. John's passionate about food, but he's not deluded.

This lack of self-delusion is a very healthy way to live. Follow your dreams. Pursue your interests with passion. But face reality. Accept that no matter how adept you are at playing shortstop in your weekend baseball game, you won't play like Derek Jeter. No matter how much applause you generated in your high school drama productions, you are not the next Meryl Streep. Most of us, when we discover that we don't have what it takes to be superstars, exhibit remarkable emotional intelligence—by accepting our limitations and moving on with our lives.

However, in my experience, no matter how emotionally sound people are when it comes to their personal lives, the delusion that they might be superstars takes on pandemic proportions in only one area: personal investing.

For reasons that defy logic, you rational people, you who would never compare yourselves to megastars, think that you can invest like the financial world's most admired pros. You believe that if you spend a few hours a week reading books, scanning the financial pages, going online to the Yahoo! Money or Motley Fool sites, and monitoring your portfolio, you too will generate annualized returns of 22 percent, as Warren Buffett has done for four decades.

Buffett, the chairman of Berkshire Hathaway, is the most enduring hero for investors—the template against which many people model their investing style and performance. He learned at the feet of a master—Ben Graham—and proceeded to build an even greater fortune. In the 1970s that "hero" could just as well have been Sir John Templeton, the humble gentleman who revolutionized international investing and created a mutual fund empire from his beachfront mansion in Lyford Cay in the Bahamas. In the 1980s that hero could have been Magellan Fund manager Peter Lynch. In the 1990s it probably was the mysterious hedge fund pioneer George Soros. Today, it may be Yale University's endowment guru, David Swenson.

All of these great investors have been hailed for their outsized returns, their consistent ability to outperform the so-called market. There is nothing wrong with that. Each has earned his reputation, his net worth, and his success.

It doesn't follow that all of us can emulate their success. Yet this delusion of easy riches within everyone's grasp refuses to die.

In a way, it's easy to explain the popularity of this delusion. The promise of personal finance magazines and the huge majority of investing books is that you too can get rich if you emulate the investing strategies of *someone who already has gotten rich.*

In a financial advice arena where the provocatively titled (e.g., Robert Allen's *Nothing Down* or Mark Hansen's *The One Minute Millionaire*) outsells the academically responsible (Jeremy Siegel's *The Future of Investors* or Ben Graham's *The Intelligent Investor*—although I suspect that Graham's work will still be read for decades to come), most books and magazines foster the dream that the average person can achieve fantastic results—and do so on autopilot. I could cite dozens of books here, but let's take one at random. My only criterion is that it has to have the word *millionaire* in the title.

Consider *The Automatic Millionaire: A Powerful One-Step Plan to Live and Finish Rich,* by financial planner David Bach. The book has an intriguing premise: Pay yourself first, and through the guaranteed wonder of compounding, you will "automatically" become a millionaire.

If you quit buying five-dollar lattes at Starbucks and save that extra cash, says Bach, your savings will eventually make you rich. Bach provides charts to show just how rich you'll become: If you bank $3,000 a year beginning at age 27, the miracle of compound interest will turn your $117,000 of savings into $1,324,777.67 by the time you are 65 and presumably ready to retire. If you begin saving at 19, a mere $24,000 investment—$3,000 a year banked for only eight years—will turn into $1,552,739.85 by the time you retire.

It's hard to dispute Bach on savings. His book is a model for thrift, an alien concept to many free-spending Americans. U.S. adults save less than anyone else in the world. In fact, our national savings rate is minus 0.6 percent, which means that collectively, we have saved nothing and are living entirely on borrowed money. The average American adult lives from paycheck to paycheck and spends beyond his or her means because of the leverage that credit cards and home equity loans provide. While citizens of other nations are obsessed with how much money they can sock away—in countries like Japan and China, where retirement plans are not emphasized, the savings rate approaches 40 percent—in the United States, people are obsessed with their credit ratings, since that determines how much more they can borrow to finance their next big purchase and how much interest they're going to have to pay on the loan. The idea of thrift has become so foreign to Americans that the wealth described in *The Automatic Millionaire* must sound like a magic formula.

But giving up a latte a day is not a formula for investment. It is a formula for saving.

I can't dispute any argument for saving. Saving is good for people. It's good for America. But what is problematic in Bach's argument can be found in the right-hand column of each of his charts. He compounds savings at a rate of 10 percent.

I do not know any savings instruments that pay 10 percent interest right now. The average money-market account pays 3 percent. With the rise in interest rates over the past few years, there are some savings accounts that actually pay as much as 5 percent. But Bach advocates investing your money in an account that will pay you 10 percent.

It was at that moment that I stopped reading, because I realized that Bach had waded into the deep end of the pool.

Is it possible to earn a steady 10 percent, year in and year out, by investing in the stock market? If you ask Wall Street "experts," they will tell you that stocks have paid a historical average return of about 11 percent, so in theory, investing in equities, either directly or in the form of mutual funds, with all of the risks involved, will indeed earn you that 11 percent. Now, an "average" 11 percent return over a long period of time doesn't sound risky, but what does the phrase *average return* really mean? It means that in some years the market rises sharply, in other years it doesn't rise at all, and some years, it actually falls. If you are able to come in at the right point in a cycle and keep your money invested long enough, goes the common belief, you will come out earning that average 11 percent. By charting investments over a lifetime—from twenty-one to sixty-five—Bach makes the numbers turn out maximally in the reader's favor. Hang in there for more than forty years, he says, and you too will be a millionaire.

I don't want to sound as if I'm picking on David Bach. What he says about savings is a truth that most people need to hear. But it's only a half-truth.

His argument falls into the category of "perfect math." It assumes that all the results are the *best* results—and that they never waver. There are no down years. No flat years. No losses.

It's no wonder that so many honest, hardworking people are deluded about their potential to be great investors. Unfortunately, the real math is far less kind.

For one thing, whether you average 11 percent depends almost entirely on *when* you enter the market. For very long periods of time markets go nowhere, and then they suddenly burst upward.

If you were lucky enough to have begun investing during, say, the burst period from 1985 to 2000, *and then managed to capture 100 percent of the gain,* you became a millionaire.

But what happens if you began to save and invest in one of those periods when the market was flat? That's where we've been since 2000. From January 1, 2000, until late 2006, the Standard & Poor's 500 advanced a miserable 0.4 percent per year. Cumulatively, if you had begun investing in the S&P 500 in 2000, you would be barely ahead from what was actually a high at the start of the decade. To achieve an average return similar to that of the period from November 1929 until the end of 1938, the Great Depression—5.6 percent—will require minimal annual returns of 15.6 percent from now until 2010. To achieve the cumulative 14.1 percent return on the S&P 500 that the decade of the Great Depression turned in, you would need to earn 19 percent on your money for the rest of the decade. Do you think that's going to happen? When stocks hit a flat period, like the one we're in now, those periods average about *twenty-five years.* So we could be stuck in this rut for as long as another two decades. If so, you'll be lucky to average 5 percent, which will turn your hoped-for millions into a few hundred thousand dollars. That's still not bad when you consider that the average free-spending American has about $10,000 in financial assets and $75,000 in home equity. But it's not enough to live on. To paraphrase the comedian Henny Youngman, most Americans have all the money they'll ever need—if they die by four o'clock this afternoon.

There is absolutely nothing "automatic" in becoming wealthy, or else everyone would do it. But the rosy assumptions and endless up cycles of a "perfect math world" are only one reason for our delusion.

Another reason is primal, emotional. We can't admit that we're mediocre at something that has been made to look so easy.

Try telling ordinary investors that they are *never* going to match the performance of the best money managers—that they are *not* going to earn the 10 percent a year they need to retire as millionaires—and you get anger, contempt, and denial in return. And sophisticates as well as the ill-informed react the same way. Recently, a colleague with world-class investment skills was forced to resign from a foundation board for suggesting to his fellow board members, who had little background in making investment decisions, that they should allow an outside manager to handle the foundation's endowment. The board members insisted that they could do the job themselves, and they were outraged that anyone would question their investing acumen.

I know these people. They would call a surgeon in the middle of the night to remove a splinter from a thumb. That's how devoted they are to expert help and advice. But when it comes to investing, they abandon common sense. They not only think they can invest, they're also convinced they can do it really well.

These are serious people. But it's hard to take them seriously when they behave like this. So if we're going to be serious about the possibility of making some money, let's begin by being honest. Let's abandon *wishing and hoping* and open ourselves up to *understanding*.

Admit this to yourself: *You will probably never be a great investor. But you might become a successful investor.*

I wish it could be otherwise. I wish that every investor could become rich. But in the zero-sum environment of most markets, where there is a buyer for every seller and a loser for every winner, it is mathematically impossible for everyone to make a killing. If it weren't, the world would be like Garrison Keillor's Lake Wobegon, where all the kids are above average. Life doesn't work that way, least of all the investing world. The gulf in the investing world between good and great is as wide as the one between great and world-class, yet nearly every one of us believes that we are the one who will bridge the gap.

The odds are stacked against you. Let's say you followed Bach's advice and put $1,000 into the S&P 500 index in 1965 and then reinvested the dividends you earned each year. By 2001 you would have built your initial investment up to $4.74 million. That's an average compound return of 11 percent, and it includes nine years when you lost money.

The problem is, real life hardly ever allows average investors to maintain the year-in, year-out discipline needed to turn a thousand dollars into $4.74 million. There is always a call on whatever money you manage to put away.

Economists and financial planners love to extol the miracle of compound investing, but there is also such a thing as compound misery, in real life and in the markets. Whether you need a down payment for a house, the kids' school payments, rising local taxes, or crises such as caring for a sick relative, covering a period of unemployment, or starting life all over again after a divorce—once you tap your investment nest egg, you can kiss your returns goodbye. You will have wound up with a scant fraction of that best possible return. You could even end up with not much more than your original thousand dollars, which, by 2005, because of inflation, would be worth a fraction of its former value.

On the other hand, let's say you were a professional investor as talented as Warren Buffett, and you had invested the same thousand dollars in Berkshire Hathaway, the company you control, over the same period. Your thousand dollars invested in 1965 would have grown to almost *$195 million* in 2005, a compound average annual growth rate of 22.6 percent. More important, if you are like Buffett, you do not have the same random trivial worries the rest of us do that siphon off your investment, because you live on a salary and make your living investing other people's money. You are a fanatic about preserving the money you control; it belongs to other people. You can't dip into Berkshire Hathaway's accumulating billions to buy the wife a new kitchen or pay for your daughter's braces or—imagine this—a squash court next to your modest home in Omaha, Nebraska! You are never scared about how long you can leave your money in the market, because you follow a rigorous investment methodology. All in all, you wind up doing *fifty* times better than the market over a lifetime. Buffett's attention to detail and commitment to making money are why he managed to prosper in an investing lifetime that included a dozen years when the markets were so dismal that *Business Week* famously predicted the "death of equities." In the 1970s, when many ordinary investors were losing their shirts, Warren Buffett had some of his best years.

You can't duplicate this performance. I don't say this to be willfully contrarian. I believe it. I'm very good at what I do, and I can't duplicate it either. If you are really going to improve your investment decision-making skills, you have to begin by accepting not only that you will never match the performance of the greatest investors, but also, quite wonderfully, that in order to become a successful investor you don't need to.

What do I mean by "successful investing"? Successful investing is making your money grow consistently by making sound decisions. Notice that I said "consistently." I didn't say "continually." One of the things that I have learned in this business is that "ten" really means "fourteen ahead and four back." Sometimes you make a lot more money than you expected, and sometimes you lose—only a little, if you are smart and quick. You do this by learning how to make your own decisions and then gaining confidence as you understand what is happening as you invest. If you blindly copy your investing heroes, you are investing without understanding—which also means that you are investing with no understanding of the risks involved. And when you spend money without factoring in the risk, you are no longer investing. You are gambling.

Odd as it may sound, I want you to lower your sights and set more realistic goals. If your goals are less foolish, you are less likely to take the foolish risks necessary to meet them. That's what I tell clients, and that's part of the message I want you to absorb. You will do better if your expectations are lower. That's not because you will convince yourself that a small return is just as good as a larger one. Rather, you will come to understand that sound decision making not only means thinking things through correctly, it also means not engaging in bad thinking. Or, putting it more simply, learning how to say no is as important as learning how to say yes. The binary of yes or no, after all, has two parts, and they are equally important.

Right now, I expect that you might be feeling a bit confused, and since I've just told you that you will probably never be a world-class investor, you are also probably a little angry and thinking to yourself, *What right does this guy have to tell me these things?* Fair enough. Part of the answer is: I'm really not much different from you.

Like many people, I didn't have a clear idea of what I wanted to do after I graduated from college. I never imagined that I was going to become a banker, let alone a global investment strategist. I graduated as a liberal arts major at Ohio Wesleyan, and then headed off to graduate school, but upon arrival there, I decided that I ought to learn something more practical. Having spent my junior year in college in Florence, Italy—and part of my junior year of high school in Norway—I was interested in learning more about how the world works. I was lucky enough to be accepted into the training course at Morgan Guaranty Trust, and ten months later I was sent to Madrid, Spain, for what was supposed to be a six-month training assignment. I arrived near the end of Franco's regime—and wound up staying six years, becoming first a witness to and then an active participant in the country's transformation into a democratic monarchy. As the number two man in a two-man office, I wound up with a lot of responsibility at a ridiculously young age and, more important, gained first-hand experience as a protagonist both witnessing and corralling unprecedented political and economic forces that forged a modern country full of investment opportunity.

That assignment led to Mexico City. Except for the language, Mexico had nothing in common with Spain. Where Spain's economy, after years of isolation, had emerged in carefully controlled steps, Mexico was in the middle of an oil boom, and the economy was already showing signs of overheating. Thanks to some highly opportune deals, our office was able to make a good deal of money for Morgan and its clients in those years, and after a decade abroad, I finally returned to New York, where I became a managing director in Morgan Guaranty/JPMorgan's Investment Management Group. I didn't create new financial products. I wasn't a globetrotting deal maker. I helped ordinary people, albeit with extraordinary resources, make money.

However, there was a problem. I could see that Wall Street firms, which are product-driven, are often in fundamental conflict with the interests of their own clients. Firms make a good part of their money from the fees they earn selling products, over and above what they charge the clients who buy them, so there is a real tendency to push products at the client, even if the product is not an appropriate fit for the client. I wanted to create a means of finding the best investments for clients, rather than simply selling them whatever the firm had to offer. Even the best firms (and Morgan remains one of the best) are limited by their product lines. I wanted more for clients. I wanted to access the best managers I knew were available. Soon thereafter I was recruited to be president of Global Asset Management, the first successful manager of manager firms. That led me to take a job with Global Asset Management, a leading multimanager investment firm that sought out the best managers from multiple sources, which gave its clients access to a much wider universe of managers, investment styles, and products. Eventually, I became president and CEO of GAM.

Still, I wasn't satisfied, and I came to believe that the best way to manage a firm from the perspective of clients was not to sell products at all. To that end I started Winter Capital International, which was strictly an advisory service that structured multimanager investment portfolios for investors. We did this by harnessing the talents of independent investment managers working all over the world. The service proved to be extremely attractive to some of the wealthiest families and investors in the world. It also proved to be extremely attractive to Citicorp, which was beefing up its private banking capabilities. In 2000, Citigroup Private Bank acquired Winter Capital, and I became the Private Bank's chief global investment strategist. In 2007, I joined Goldman Sachs.

Through all of these career moves, I have maintained a belief that every investor is entitled to the best advice available. Obviously, the more resources an investor has, the better the advice he or she is generally going to get. I say this with some trepidation, because many very wealthy people get a lot of poor advice from the people who invest their money for them.

At this point, I have learned not to deal in products at all, but rather in investment ideas. Nowadays, I have the privilege of spending time in New York and around the world, either *listening* or *talking*.

I listen to clients, colleagues, investment bankers, money managers, entrepreneurs, CEOs, regulatory officers, and government leaders, al-

ways on the alert for their views about what's going on in their corners of
the world.

When I talk, it's usually in the form of formal presentations to clients
and managers in which I synthesize and share what I have learned.

The bulk of this book is my attempt to recapture and reformulate what
I have been telling bankers and high-net-worth clients over the past
decade, helping them comprehend the most obvious and elusive investing concept of all—*opportunity*.

To make my form of binary decision making work for you, you have to
understand a few things. First, there is no right or wrong in a binary. You
are assessing information, and you are also assessing how *other* people
think about the binary. Remember: in investing, there is a buyer for every
seller, a loser for every winner. Your job is to figure out which way a bit of
information points you. Is it telling you to buy? Or is it saying sell? Is a bit
of information you've learned encouraging you to put your money to work,
or is it telling you to stay on the sidelines? And when I say "you," I don't
mean some theoretical other person. The circumstances that make an investment opportunity right for one individual can make the same investment opportunity terrible for another. It is *your* job to absorb the
information, put it against the binary, and then make the decision that is
right for you.

Identifying opportunity begins with a binary I call *certainty versus uncertainty*. This binary deals with risk, or, really, decision making when
not all of the facts are known. I present this certainty/uncertainty binary
to clients in the chart on the next page, diagramming the relationship
between what is *knowable and understandable* (that's certainty) and
what is *unknown and unforeseeable* (that's uncertainty) to show that these
polar opposites can lead to something in between, namely the *visible yet
incomprehensible*—which is where opportunity lies.

When we know and understand what's going on in the world—that's
certainty—traditional equity investing works quite well. Your choices of
where to invest can be made purely on the basis of whose balance sheet is
best and whose prospects are rising. That's the way the world operated
from about 1985 to 2000. That's when most investors came into the mar-

Knowable and
Understandable

Unknown and
Unforeseeable

Visible yet
Incomprehensible

ket, and so they came to believe that the market would always behave that way.

But that's wrong. Often, we are blindsided by the unknown and the unforeseeable. In a word, *uncertainty.*

Just look at the past several years: Who could have predicted the subprime crisis, al-Qaeda's attacks on New York and Washington, the collapse of the Internet and telecom bubbles, the accounting scandals that brought down Arthur Andersen, WorldCom, Enron, and a host of other companies, *and* Hurricane Katrina's destruction of New Orleans? Sure, some smart person might have intuited one of these events, perhaps even two. There were, after all, signs of vulnerability and evidence of misfeasance up and down the line for all of these disasters. But we generally train ourselves to ignore such signs and bet on normalcy and happy endings. With hurricanes, we've seen them before. Terrorism is something we've seen enough of on television, but always someplace else. Never here, we believed. And of course, there is our abiding faith in numbers and our own accounting rules and regulations, which blinded us both to the stock market bubbles that were about to burst and to the financial misdeeds that would fill the headlines the past few years.

Most of the time, it is neither the knowable nor the unforeseen that eludes us. It is the information that is *visible yet incomprehensible.* We see the evidence of a tsunami on television, but who knows what it means to the economies of East Asia? You're not an economist, so how do you know whether you can profit from investing in these economies or should avoid them? You know that the telecom bubble burst and that there are tens of thousands of miles of so-called dark fiber—fiber-optic cable that was feverishly installed between 1998 and 2000 in the hopes of a continually rising Internet economy soaking up bandwidth. But you are not a telecom analyst, so you don't know whether or not to buy the cable and telecom companies that own the fiber and are patiently waiting for demand to meet supply.

That which is visible yet incomprehensible supplies much of the possibility of opportunity. Let's be more blunt about it: the ability to get more information on such situations—to make them more comprehensible—is what creates opportunity for investors. Much of this information is at your disposal. It's in the newspapers, on the Web, and in the minds of experts down the street or a phone call away. Often, good knowledge exists in reference books available in any library. Such information will not automatically make you a better investor, but it can help you sharpen your decision processes.

The reality is that rich people make more money because they are skilled at evaluating information quickly, and in then deciding how to act on what they've learned. While you are worrying about your life of imminent poverty if you guess wrong with the family nest egg, savvy investors have already plunged in and secured their superior returns.

This notion of binary thinking is not only how I see the world, it's how the smartest people I meet see it as well. They shrink their decision making into simple either/or choices, not just in investing but everywhere else as well.

Most great CEOs give the impression that they have attention deficit disorder. They appear to be impatient and prone to making decisions that seem hurried, if not outright random. To the practiced eye, that impression is false. Successful CEOs no more have ADD than the rest of the population. They are extremely busy and mildly overcommitted. They have a lot on their plates. As a result, they tend to cast their decisions as simple either/or, yes/no choices. They don't have the time to sort through enormous amounts of data. True, they have staffs to perform that task, but in the end, they use a set of binary indicators to make decisions, whether they have all the facts or not.

As you familiarize yourself with the binaries to come, you'll see that they address much larger issues than the standard questions about a company's management or its P/E ratios or its next quarter's outlook or how many analysts have labeled the company *buy, sell,* or *hold.* If you can address these binary issues first, deciding whether opportunity or entitlement is more important, or whether it's the wired world or the wireless one that deserves more investment, or whether preservation or growth strategies should prevail, for example, the standard questions will become secondary (although still vital)—because you'll now know whether you need to investigate further or simply move on.

When you learn to understand these pairs, it won't matter that your surname isn't Buffett, Soros, Lynch, or Swenson. It won't matter if you are exposed to the best deals or not. You will have learned to see the world as an endless number of viable investments that you might or might not want to participate in. The choice is up to you. But at least you'll know what the options are. They're as simple as fear or greed, alpha or beta, wired or wireless, preservation or growth. This alone puts you far ahead of nearly everyone else. In a world where a problem well stated is a problem half solved, that clarity of choice improves your odds when you risk your money.

There are so many different ways to invest money—more than fifteen thousand publicly traded companies worldwide, almost as many mutual funds, thousands of hedge funds, and endless commodity, option, currency, and bond products—that you ought to be able to find many that work well for you. Learning to open your mind to the possibilities will help you narrow the differences between yourself and the best professional investors.

I also want to help you avoid bad managers, the hordes on Wall Street who are only in it for the money they can make for themselves, not for their clients. The fact is, even if you are a smart investor, you can easily get taken in by a good sales pitch or by the appearance of good results. I once had a client who died, and his widow, while she was intelligent and had helped to build his business, knew nothing about investing. When she came to me for help, we interviewed a number of investment advisors, and at the end of the second day, she said, "You know, I understand now why I'm the solution to all these managers' problems. I just don't know how any of *them* is going to be the solution to *my* problem."

More than anything else, I want you to become more self-reliant as an investor.

I would like to help you to become a little bit smarter about how money works—and perhaps a little more confident that you can make it work for you.

Now, let's begin.

FIRST, DON'T BREAK THESE FOUR RULES

Before you can think for yourself, you have to reorient your thinking about the "investment industry." That's the giant complex of financial institutions, media channels, and businesses that earn their profits from your investments. It's a vast noise machine, and I've been part of it for thirty years. So before you immerse yourself in binary decision making, here are four rules to help you navigate the investment industry, lest you fall victim to clever sales pitches or your own hubris.

RULE 1. DON'T LOSE MONEY.

A physician is taught, "First, do no harm." It's the same in investing.

Every broker or fund manager has something to sell you, with the implied promise that you will make money. There are legal disclaimers in tiny print at the end of every investment solicitation that warn you that you might lose money, but no broker or mutual fund salesman ever trumpets that fact when he is trying to sell you a product. If your job were investing money and you knew that your bonus, your home, and your family's welfare depended upon it, you would probably become a better investor immediately. The prospect of losing everything in a financial beheading (to pilfer from Samuel Johnson on the prospect of hanging) concentrates the mind wonderfully.

But making money is not your day job. It's something that matters to you, for sure. But so does not missing your kid's soccer game.

The hard truth is: *you don't make your money work for you because you don't take the job of not losing money seriously enough.*

"Don't lose money" sounds like that Will Rogers maxim, "Only buy stocks that go up." But it's actually more profound (and not nearly as obvious).

For one thing, it helps you understand risk. If you have $10,000 in the market in a given year and you lose half of it on a bad investment—$5,000—then, in order to break even the next year, you have to earn a 100 percent return on the money that remains. Now, over decades, the S&P 500 basket of large-cap stocks earned an average of 11.6 percent, and over that same period Buffett earned 22 percent. But remember: since the beginning of this decade, the S&P 500 has risen only 0.4 percent annually, so you are going to have to make your investments grow at 19 percent annually just to have an *average* return for the rest of the decade. To do that you'd have to be almost as good as the best. That's just not likely.

It also helps you understand the value of principal accumulation. You know that stocks rise and fall. So the best way not to lose money is not to buy stocks, at least not right away. Begin by learning to save. Put your nest-egg money into bonds or principal-protected notes and begin accumulating interest. If you do that for several years, you will have three things: a thrift habit, a useful nest egg, and a chunk of money in the form of interest with which you can begin to invest. All of these, especially the thrift habit, are good. If you are stashing money in an IRA or SEP account, you can build up a sizable balance, the interest from which you can begin to use in your investment forays, without immediate tax consequences. If you lose some of the interest, that is the price of learning. The trick is to not lose the nest-egg principal and, in fact, to keep adding to it while you are investing the interest. If you constantly add to the principal and invest cautiously and then reinvest the interest, you will do fairly well. In fact, you could do nothing more than that, if you have the discipline, and stop reading now.

And remember what I said: getting ahead 10 percent often means getting ahead more than that and then losing some. Everyone wants to make money continually. The trick is to make it consistently and to accept the fact that sometimes you are going to make a bad decision. What you want to do is make fewer bad ones and more good ones. This law of averages governs almost everything we do. A baseball player who guesses wrong on which pitch to hit two times out of three—in other words, someone who fails with great consistency—still has a great shot at the Hall of Fame as a .333 hitter. An NBA star like Michael Jordan can miss half his shots and still wind up as one of the all-time greats. You need to be able to make the right decision just a little more than half the time to become a sound investor.

RULE 2. DON'T INVEST WHERE BIG INVESTORS INVEST.

If you read *Barron's* or *Forbes* or the *New York Times* Sunday business section, there is always a column in which some bright investment manager or some rich investor is asked what he or she recommends. If you follow their recommendations, you might do well, but not as well as they're going to do. They already own the stocks they're recommending, and they want you to come in and bump up the price by creating artificial demand. There are lots of studies showing that when a stock is written about in a positive way in one of the major financial publications, the short-term price can be pushed up for a week or so, until the next "recommendation" from the next money manager comes out. Then the stock falls as everyone rushes into the next recommendation. The money manager who issued the recommendation has in all likelihood already put in his sell orders, so that when you begin buying, he's collecting his gain off your back. So resist the urge to follow the crowd.

But people make the same mistake even when they are not falling prey to any of this standard market mischief.

I always wince when I hear people say that they've bought shares in a company because they read that a famous investor has been accumulating the stock. The only problem with this copycat investing, of course, is that investors have no idea what the investor they're reading about paid for his stock or when he bought the shares. It's a bit like copying a great chef's recipe from a torn page that's missing half the ingredients and all the cooking instructions.

RULE 3. FIND A WATERFALL AND PUT YOUR BUCKET UNDER IT.

George Soros said that most investors look for a pond where they can put their buckets, but most ponds are shallow and dry up quickly. Instead, he advised, find a waterfall and place your bucket under it. Whether it is a slow drip or a mighty torrent, your bucket will fill and refill.

Ponds? Buckets? Waterfalls? I don't mean to sound gnomic or Zen-like. But there are two countervailing theories in investing. The first says, diversify your assets and spread your risk. The second says, in Mark Twain's version, put all your eggs in one basket and closely *watch* the basket. Soros, in effect, is saying the latter. So am I. It is easier to learn and master one thing than to try to master dozens of things about which you know very little. The latter will trap you into investing without full knowledge.

Although the investment industry is built on the first formula—asset allocation—every legendary investor follows the second formula. The only variable (and it's a big variable) is where they put their bucket. Warren Buffett, for example, is known as a "value investor." He has a formula that he learned fifty years ago when he was a student of Benjamin Graham, the Columbia University professor and fund manager who created a mechanism for defining undervalued companies. Buffett follows the Graham formula religiously when he invests. That's his waterfall.

George Soros built his fortune by learning how the currency markets work and by being able to discern the relationships between global politics and currency behavior so that he could use leverage to place enormous bets on currency movements. That's his waterfall.

Peter Lynch, of Fidelity's Magellan Fund fame, discerned in the 1970s that America was changing and becoming a more prosperous consumer society and made money by investing in consumer stocks that had been stagnant for years. That was his waterfall.

Sir John Templeton discovered international investing before anyone else and put his bucket into the huge waterfall of emerging stock markets.

Larry Tisch, another savvy investor, discovered that there was a completely different kind of value in companies than can be revealed by Graham's formula. Tisch looked for firms that spend too much on nonsense, like company jets, and then bought them, wrung out the excesses, and collected the torrent of profits that fell to the bottom line.

PIMCO's Bill Gross found his waterfall in bonds. He mastered the intricacies of the yield curve and put his bucket there, making huge returns on very small movements in the bond market.

Each successful investor found a single gushing waterfall and placed his bucket under it.

Of course, you could be cynical and say that those investment styles worked for their inventors but not as well for others, because they were the first in. I'll concede that good returns plus good public relations equals a legendary reputation, but you're not trying to become an investment legend. You're trying to make enough money so you can retire comfortably. You don't need to earn 22 percent annually. All you need for a comfortable retirement is to do better than the rate of inflation, whatever it happens to be, plus another 5 or 6 percent to make your money grow in real terms.

It doesn't matter what your waterfall is; you just want to find one that you're comfortable with and then fill your bucket. It could be real estate, or it could be investing in automobile stocks. (Yes, auto stocks. Despite the low esteem in which Wall Street holds them, auto stocks do go up from time to time. Look at General Motors. In 2005 it was all but written off. Since then, as the company has begun to make itself over, investors have pushed the stock up by more than a third. Ford is another story entirely!) Whatever it is, master an investment discipline, and you will gradually and steadily see your returns improve.

The same goes for mastering one industry. Each of us, if only through the specialized knowledge we acquire in our jobs, has the opportunity to be an expert at something. If you can acquire world-class knowledge of one sector of the economy, you can sit under a waterfall.

Consider that the complex global economy is built on oil. Oil is one of the most thoroughly researched and documented industries I can think of. Almost any piece of information you need to know about oil can be found with one or two keystrokes of your computer. If you turned yourself into an amateur oil expert, you would uncover some compelling investment choices that are invisible to your friends and neighbors.

For example, most investors have known for more than a year that refinery capacity is constrained in the United States and around the world and that oil and gasoline prices will head upward at any sign of a squeeze on supply. Oil prices jumped after the United States invaded Iraq, and they jumped again when both Nigeria and Venezuela had political problems that temporarily shut off their oil shipments.

Now, you could have made money, as a lot of investors did, just by buying the stocks of the large oil companies, since their profit margins go up whenever the price of a barrel of oil rises. Why? They have long-term contracts with the oil-producing countries and pay a "lifting fee" that is only a fraction of the market price of a barrel of oil. If the price of oil rises in the marketplace, the country earns more and the company that lifted the oil earns more. Not surprisingly, oil stocks have been leading market performers since mid-2004.

But there were other ways to make more money from oil than buying the oil majors. Because demand was rising—not only does the United States want more oil, but so do China and much of the developing world—you could have made money by purchasing the shares of the handful of shipping companies that own the tankers that ship all the world's oil. Why? Because of a series of catastrophic oil spills over the past decade, world environmental law has mandated that oil be shipped in double-hulled tankers, which are in short supply. Shipping companies, meanwhile, are trying to minimize the extra insurance costs of shipping oil in single-hulled tankers by scrapping them at an accelerating rate, but the new double-hulled ships have been slow to come out of the shipyards into service. The result: a shortage of tankers, which leads to higher shipping rates, which leads to much higher profits for the shipping companies, which leads to higher share prices.

There's more. The nations that produce oil—OPEC and non-OPEC alike—have been taking in more revenue, most of which enters national treasuries. This money—all of it in dollars, as that is the way oil is priced and traded in international markets—makes the currencies of the oil producers worth more, as the ratio of foreign exchange holdings to their own currency in circulation begins to drop. The Mexican peso, for example, has appreciated more than 20 percent against the dollar since the price of oil began rising in 2004. Other currencies, such as the Saudi riyal, have shown similar gains. By purchasing a couple of contracts on the peso or the riyal—which you can buy for a fraction of the cost of buying shares in a company—you could have made 20 percent or more for yourself, with very little risk. Admittedly, that's a slightly more sophisticated investment maneuver than plunking spare cash into an index fund, but enough people have taken that route that today, $1.9 trillion—that's *trillion*—worth of currency contracts are traded each day, a rise of 60 percent since 2001. Or, if you are too timid for currency trading, you could have bought Mexican Cetes—the short-term bonds the Mexican government issues to balance its budget—and gotten both a higher interest rate than comparable U.S. Treasury issues *and* the kicker of currency appreciation.

Indeed, there were a couple dozen ways to make money off the rise in the price of oil. Each one was its own distinct waterfall, perhaps not a Niagara but powerful nonetheless. Every single one of these investments requires nothing more than a bit of knowledge, some careful study, and the willingness to make a decision.

RULE 4. OPEN YOUR MIND.

This rule is as important as the first three combined.

You won't be able to see a waterfall if you are only looking at one type of investment. For decades, Americans have put all their money into "long-only" directional strategies, jargon for buy-and-hold equity investments. Most Americans have put their money almost exclusively into U.S. stocks that they hold, even when the market goes down, in expectation that at some point, the market will go back up to new heights. That's the way it was between 1985 and 2000, when most of the current generation of Americans came into the market. Fifteen years is a lifetime for most investors.

The United States, though, is now only a small part, about a third by gross domestic product, of a much larger and increasingly wealthy world beyond our shores. Some smart people have already figured this out, and Americans now put about a sixth of their money into foreign shares, usually through region- or country-specific mutual funds.

That's a terrific start at taking a broader view on investing, but it's just a start.

As an example of what I mean about keeping an open mind, let's take the recent example of Hurricane Katrina—and its economic implications.

The Friday before Katrina hit, I was in my office watching a news program, and a commentator was talking about how people were boarding up their homes and how this was probably a good time to buy Home Depot stock. One of my colleagues in the office with me said, "Wrong lesson. If Katrina hits New Orleans, the city is going to be under water. The thing to buy is a digital camera. Take pictures of everything you own, grab your titles and deeds, your insurance policies and checkbook, head to an ATM machine, and then get out of town."

He was right, as it turned out. The plywood-on-the-windows drill, which is the typical Florida response, proved useless in New Orleans and along much of the Gulf Coast. The people who are going to recover the fastest are the people who have a little money and their papers and those photographs of their possessions. They will get close to a hundred cents on the dollar from their insurance policies, and they will recover more quickly than those who were nailing boards on their windows. Remember, the first rule is "Don't lose money." Taking the proper precautions is the best way to avoid coming out on the short end.

The same colleague, the following Tuesday, after the storm had struck with its full fury, said, "Forget Home Depot and Lowe's. That's for repairs. Buy the stocks of mobile home companies, because New Orleans is going to be flattened and people are going to be living in trailers for years on end." He was right again. FEMA soon announced plans to purchase and distribute upwards of 300,000 trailers and mobile homes to house the displaced of Louisiana and Mississippi.

There are lots of rules for investors, but these are the only four you'll need as you read on. When you combine the wisdom in these rules with the decision-making options contained within the binaries, you will have learned how to turn information into opportunity.

One more word about the binaries: I am going to put them into three frameworks. The first I call "A Changing World." Investment decision making today is different than it was only five or six years ago. Learning how it has changed and how it is likely to shift in the future is an important component of learning how to find opportunity in uncertainty. The second framework is "A Changing Investor." You are not the same as you were five years ago. Americans are getting older, diminishing their appetite for risk. At the same time, your investments have probably been injured to a certain extent, so there is even more pressure on you to make them turn out well than there was five years ago. Next, we examine "A Changing Market." You can't afford just to be on Wall Street anymore, and you can't afford to look at stocks only. The world has globalized, and you have to globalize your investments to get better returns, as opportunity has increasingly shifted offshore and into investments much less straightforward than buying the stock of one or two companies and then holding on for life. It's not even as clear-cut as buying sector-specific mutual funds. Finally, I am going to look at a few binaries that present new opportunities, potential new waterfalls under which you can place your bucket. I'm not going to do your work for you, but I will tell you a few ways to start.

PART I

A CHANGING WORLD

Drivers, Passengers, and Roadkill

All successful investors have in their minds what the Germans call a *Weltanschauung,* a view of the world and the forces that contribute to shaping it. When I visit with clients and bankers, I bring my worldview with me, and my remarks are made within its context. I won't make the claim that my view is right and that others are wrong; it's just that without a lens through which to view events, it is extremely difficult to make decisions about investment opportunities. You see, it is possible for people to have different worldviews and still make money, but it is nearly impossible to make money consistently without a worldview.

A worldview must be wide, not narrow. If you think a set of prejudices constitutes a worldview, you are wrong. Things change. People change. Yesterday's struggling nations may be tomorrow's powerhouses, yesterday's allies may become tomorrow's enemies, and vice versa. If you are going to become a successful investor, you have to erase the phrase *It will never happen* from your lexicon. If you live long enough, the world will turn upside down, perhaps even a couple of times. Successful investing begins with learning about the world. That means picking up a couple of good newspapers, such as *The New York Times* or *The Washington Post* or the *Financial Times,* and reading them on a regular basis. Reading the world and national news along with some business news will make you better informed and give you information that will help you support your view of the world as it develops. You should also be reading magazines and journals such as *The Economist* and *Foreign Affairs*—again, not so that you can become an expert on the world, but so that when you do see an investment opportunity, you will have frames of reference against which to measure it. (I should note that all of these newspapers and journals have their own world-views and biases, and you should be aware of them, but you are reading more for information than opinion. Most of the time, you won't even notice the biases in the news sections.)

Since I read these publications and subscribe to some very high-priced information services, when I get information, I take it in and organize it. I have noticed that most information can be put into a couple of major buckets that I am interested in at any given time, and every time I see a story that is even remotely related to one of the buckets, or themes, I cut it out and put it into a file. You don't have to do that. You can rely upon your memory, if it's good, or put a couple of articles aside, since you are not making investment decisions at the same level that I do. But since good investment decision making is ultimately backed up by facts and is not solely based upon opinions or hunches, · any kind of system that allows you to lay your hands on the facts will help you. If you want to get really obsessive about this process, read *Off the Record: What Wall Street Doesn't Want You to Know,* by Craig Gordon, published in 2001. His San Francisco firm, Off-the-Record Research, does extremely detailed digging on companies for their Wall Street investment clients. His book explains how to emulate his methods, and, just as important, it explains the value of smart research in investment decision making. I don't do anything nearly as complex, but with just a worldview and a little information, I can make out pretty well.

As new evidence comes along, revisit the assumptions that you are making about how the world works and how and when you should invest. A change in facts should lead you to adjust your view from time to time—usually in small ways, but once in a while in a major way. What do we mean by *world*? For years, in many circles the phrase *the world* did not mean the entire planet and all of its people, but rather a narrow world within a world that took shape after World War II in a series of · agreements on trade, monetary policy, and exchange rates. This smaller world and its rules did not govern the entire planet; rather, it governed only the signatories to the treaties that created it. For people who lived within this rarefied, closed-off portion of the greater world, it was as if the political freedoms that went along with this world were coupled to economic freedoms that made companies and investors unremittingly optimistic. If you went to the larger world outside, you would feel the crushing weight of regulations and oppression that made investing all but impossible.

This smaller world was the world according to GATT, the General Agreement on Tariffs and Trade, which was signed by twenty-three nations in 1947. GATT, which eventually grew to 125 signatories before it was replaced by the World Trade Organization in 1995, helped to define the world economy and its rules of trade. For currencies and exchange rates, this small special world began with the Bretton Woods Agreements in 1944, while World War II was still raging. They created a system of fixed exchange rates backed by convertibility into gold. In 1971, the Bretton Woods system of fixed rates abruptly collapsed when the United States, pressured by France, decided that it would no longer repay dollars with gold. Since then, we have lived in a world of floating currencies. That change, from fixed to floating currencies, was the first great shock to the postwar worldview that had been constructed by America and its allies.

This smaller world was also the world governed by the Federal Reserve. After World War II, with Europe and Japan prostrate, the only thing holding the world together was the U.S. dollar and the willingness of Americans to spend. For members of the world of GATT and Bretton Woods, that willingness was embodied in the Marshall Plan, the World Bank, and the International Monetary Fund, institutions either wholly or largely funded by the United States. The Federal Reserve System, America's central bank, had come into being as the result of the destruction of one worldview and the start of a new one, which would prevail until the end of World War II. The Federal Reserve System was established in 1912 as a direct result of the Panic of 1907, a brief interlude that began exactly eighteen months after the San Francisco earthquake, when the United States literally ran out of money and had to import a boatload of borrowed gold from England to re-monetize its currency. The new central bank that emerged from that crisis decided to avoid the possibility of parts of the country running out of money by breaking the United States into a dozen regions and issuing currency according to the needs of each region, as measured by commercial and bank activity and so forth. As time went on, the Fed's role evolved into using the money supply to regulate the economy and, later, using interest rates to regulate the money supply. When there was too much money in circulation, the Fed would raise rates to make borrowing for expansion more expensive and thus more difficult. When the economy cooled, the Fed would lower rates to make borrowing easier.

Why is this economic and institutional history important, even in abbreviated form? Because the influence of the U.S. Federal Reserve within the world that the United States and its allies and trading partners had created for itself in the wake of World War II became the thermostat for everyone within that world, raising and lowering the economic heat according to the needs of the U.S. economy. It was as if all of the participants had put on special blinders that allowed them not to see the rising populations of China, India, and the old Soviet bloc, which among them contained 60 percent of the world's people, most of whom were mired in poverty despite immense natural resources. While a number of thoughtful leaders made noises about bringing those areas into "our" world, most of us were content to ignore what was going on beyond our boundaries.

For companies and investors who lived inside "our" world, success meant learning how to interpret the actions of the Fed and relating those actions to the movements of interest rates and currencies and, indirectly, stocks and bonds. From the end of World War II until perhaps a decade ago, investment theory was directly tied to what the Federal Reserve did with interest rates. The Fed had become the de facto "driver" of our corner of the world, and countries, companies, and investors who learned how to put on yet another set of more subtle blinders, this time directed solely at the Fed and its behavior, became successful "passengers." That is, as long as they adjusted correctly to the Fed's dictates, they made money. When the Federal Reserve lowered interest rates, corporate passengers invested in their companies through capital spending and innovation, which led astute individual investors to invest in stocks. When the Fed raised interest rates, individuals pulled their money out of the equity markets in favor of bonds and companies paid down their debts and used the time to prune corporate deadwood, in the form of unprofitable divisions, products that didn't sell, or, sometimes, employees.

The passengers to the Fed's drivers learned to distinguish what was important from what mattered less or not at all. If the Federal Reserve was the major driver inside our world, then Fed-watching, interpreting the comments of whoever was the Fed chairman, became critical to determining what investment decisions to make, both as individuals and as companies. For nearly sixty years, this worldview prevailed, bringing with it prosperity and order. But even as that world was approaching its zenith, the seeds of change had already been planted.

The Johnny Appleseed of global change was President Nixon. Though the judgment of history is still out on him, Nixon's 1972 visit to China and the changes that ultimately brought reformist Deng Xiaoping to power in 1978 set in motion the modern world as we know it. Nixon recognized the several billion people who were outside the existing global system, and he realized that if they could somehow be brought into it, American business would benefit. Nixon and Kissinger, his secretary of state, were pragmatists who believed that only trade and normalization, not democratic rhetoric, would change China.

While China began to go slowly but steadily down the path of reform, change was also beginning to take root in the Soviet Union. British prime minister Margaret Thatcher, acting on sound intelligence, finally figured out what nobody else in the West wanted to admit: that the USSR was nothing more than a tottering Potemkin village, a long-failed state, albeit one with nuclear missiles. The trick was persuading the Soviets to accept that fact, and while President Reagan's famous "Mr. Gorbachev, tear down this wall" speech in June 1987 is credited with beginning the end of the Cold War, a closer reading of the full text of the speech reveals that the Soviets had also begun to take steps down the path of reform.

Since 1989, with the fall of the Berlin Wall, the end of the Soviet Union, the dissolution of the old Soviet empire, and the emergence of several dozen states into the sunlight of freedom and economic liberalism, these states, with a wobble here and a currency crisis there, have slowly taken their place as actors on the world stage, and the flow of capital around the world has changed dramatically as a consequence. While the Fed was once at the monetary center of the world, now it is but one player among many. The European Central Bank has become a coequal player, and the People's Bank of China is also now a force to be reckoned with.

Another change that is going to have a long-term impact on the world is that the West has become credit-dependent while the rest of the world is just beginning to experience the use of credit. While allocating credit more fairly is useful in stimulating growth, and while the development of tools such as securitization have spurred that growth to unprecedented heights, the entire world now watches with alarm as the United States and Europe have to cope with the impact of the subprime mortgage crisis and the severe tightening of other credit markets, which, as of this writing, might yet drag the United States and the rest of the world into a severe recession. There is nothing inherently wrong with the extension of credit, and much that is right; the problems of credit arise out of a combination of corporate and political greed and shortsightedness. In paying more attention to quarterly profits than to the creditworthiness of their customers, some banks, it appears, began selling products solely for the fees they could collect, and then repackaging those products and reselling them for yet more profits. By packaging them with options and default swaps (to make them more attractive, by lowering perceived risk) and then slicing bundled mortgages into multiple tranches, each of which carried the rating of the best mortgages in the tranche, a multitrillion dollar industry was created, one that was further fueled by falling interest rates and a benign Fed.

The politicians got into the act long before the current credit crisis began. At the turn of the twentieth century, politicians used to promise voters a "chicken in every pot," coded language for pay levels such that everyone could eat well. By the end of the century, that promise could have been "a credit card in every wallet." Credit shifted from a privilege earned to an entitlement owed, and as politicians pushed the Fed and the banks to extend credit to more and more people, they obliged by creating products that provided money to people who had less and less capacity to repay. All that was fine as long as interest rates continued to fall, as they generally did for the twenty-year period beginning in the early 1980s, and as long as other nations were willing to finance American debt so that Americans would continue to buy products imported from rising Asian and European economies.

But something had to give. When subprime and adjustable-rate mortgages began to reset in 2006, the entire game began to come apart, and the Fed, with few arrows in its quiver at that point—it was still pumping liquidity into the U.S. market in an attempt to keep it prosperous, while money flowed out at an even faster rate to pay for the war in Iraq—could do nothing to forestall a growing number of mortgage foreclosures and home abandonments. Foreigners, who had been financing much of the rising U.S. credit debt, became alarmed, and when your creditor gets scared, be alert! The dollar began a slow descent that is in danger of becoming a cascade from great heights. Commodities priced in dollars, like gold, corn, and oil, are suddenly reaching historic highs, and while other components of the credit market are still holding up, there is a fear, which will not go away until it goes away, that what has happened in the U.S. housing market will happen in other credit markets.

In this new world, not only the foreigners who have long invested in dollars are going to be looking to diversify; Americans will as well. Unfortunately, we are still slow on the uptake.

The up-and-downness of some foreign countries can be discouraging for investors, especially since we Americans seem to know little about geography and even less about world events. Even sophisticated investors are often loath to venture into unknown territory. The 2006 edition of the "World Wealth Report," an annual publication of Merrill Lynch and Capgemini, a consulting firm, dryly notes that "despite a gradual shift over the past few years, North American high-net-worth individuals remained significantly invested in—and more narrowly focused on—domestic markets, with a heavy weighting of United States–centric investments." Despite a falling dollar and dismal returns by U.S. stocks across the board, Americans kept their money at home.

CHAPTER 1

THE DEVELOPED *versus* THE DEVELOPING WORLD WORLD

The developed world has people with money to spend. The developing world, meanwhile, has endless needs and a growing pool of savings. Which will be the better investment in the years ahead? The developed world has aging populations who will increasingly have to save for retirement and who will have to be parsimonious if they are going to have enough money to last their entire lives. Does that make them a bad investment? Not at all. Citizens of the developed world enjoy long life, and the willingness to spend money on health care treatments, leisure activities, and life experiences such as travel, hotels, and restaurants—all this makes for good investing in certain sectors. Just look at the cosmetic surgery market: at one time it was limited almost exclusively to older women. Women still account for most cosmetic procedures, but men are making up more of the total than they used to. In 2005, men underwent 13 percent of all procedures, according to the American Society for Aesthetic Plastic Surgery, up from 11.7 percent in 2002 and 9.7 percent in 1998. The total number of cosmetic procedures increased 18 percent in 2005, to 7.2 million. What's more, increasingly those procedures are being done by for-profit surgicenters connected not to hospitals but rather to hotel and spa chains, where patients can recover at their leisure, in pleasant surroundings. According to a July 2006 article in the *Los Angeles Times*, various companies are preparing to build as many as fifteen thousand of these stand-alone centers in the United States and Canada over the next ten years.

Over in the developing world, medicine of a different kind is an equally good bet. Health care budgets in many nations are rising rapidly, and as countries pass out of the infectious-disease phase of health care, the budget is increasingly spent on the management of chronic illnesses, such as diabetes, hypertension, and heart disease, and on modern instrumentation, such as CT scanners and MRI devices. These are all made by a handful of U.S. and European firms, so as health care globalizes, opportunities for investors develop.

But health care is just one part of the puzzle. For years, public infrastructure spending in developed nations stagnated, while most of the action was in the developing world. No longer. The infrastructure of much of the United States and Europe is aging and obsolete and needs to be replaced: roads, dams, bridges, tunnels, even whole cities. The money for these projects comes from municipal financing, which, because of a rising interest rate environment, will result in higher rates on municipal bonds, which are generally tax-free, or, increasingly, through private equity deals that transfer ownership of public property to investors and take them off the tax rolls, allowing politicians to hold the line on raising taxes. Either way, there is sure to be a windfall for the manufacturers of the equipment that reshapes and rebuilds the infrastructure. Some of those companies will be American, but the steel is likely to come from China, Brazil, Korea, South Africa, or Mexico. The cement will come from an Italian, French, or Mexican company—a decade ago they bought up most of their American competitors—and the technology will just as likely come from a German or Japanese firm as an American one.

So is it the developing world or the developed? The answer depends upon the opportunity. If you had to pick between, say, a 30-year airport expansion bond paying 5 percent offered by a U.S. entity such as the Port Authority of New York and New Jersey, or a 30-year Mexican municipal bond from the state of Quintana Roo with a coupon of 7 percent, the answer would appear to be a no-brainer. The Mexican bond pays a higher interest rate, and at the same time the Mexican peso continues to appreciate against the dollar, giving you the possibility of earning 8 or 9 percent. But wait. The Port Authority has been paying off bonds successfully since 1921 and has never missed a payment even though it has no power to tax and must pay bondholders with the revenues it earns by managing bridges, tunnels, ports, and airports in and around New York and New

Jersey. The Mexican state of Quintana Roo, on the other hand, has no prior history of municipal borrowing, and while Mexico is currently in the midst of an economic upsurge, there are no guarantees that that will continue. Indeed, the disputed 2006 national election may create bitterness despite the outcome and may prejudice investors against Mexico for some time to come. So what you really have to decide is whether you are being adequately compensated for the risk you are taking whenever you make an investment.

There are bond-rating agencies that are supposed to help you answer that question, and you can go to your local public library and look up the Quintana Roo bond or get the rating from your broker or from the Internet. You can look at all three ratings—Fitch, Standard & Poor's, and Moodys—in a matter of seconds, and generally you will find that most of the rating agencies are in accord with one another. But don't be fooled. The agencies generally rate the risk for the bond only at the time of issue and depend upon the markets to reprice the bond thereafter, unless a *significant* piece of news forces them to rerate the bond. If, for example, Mexico's government were to turn sharply leftward, the rating agencies, fearing repudiation, might lower the bond's rating, even if Quintana Roo had remained scrupulous about making its interest payments.

Generally, you will notice that investors who commit to globalizing their portfolios are a cautious lot. Brazil's economy is roaring ahead, to be sure, but even though Brazil's Bovespa index has more than tripled over the past five years, Brazilian stocks still have low P/E ratios compared to U.S. stocks. In other words, they are undervalued by American standards, often by half or more, even though the companies are turning in double-digit growth rates. Why? It is because investors look at Brazil and see a long history of booms followed by significant declines. Fiscal discipline seems to take hold in Brazil for a few years and then vanish again like Brigadoon, not to reappear for another generation. Enough investors have been burned in the past by investing in Brazil that many remain skeptical about just how long the current honeymoon will last, and it is hard to fault them. Brazil's current president, Luis Inácio da Silva, known as "Lula," is a former leftist trade unionist who courageously took the step of adopting middle-of-the-road economic policies just at the time when

China's commodity-dependent economy was moving into high gear. The combination of sound fiscal management and booming exports has driven Brazil's chronic inflation down to near normal levels, has added billions of dollars to the nation's foreign exchange reserves, and has raised the living standards of Brazil's growing urban population. But you have to ask yourself how much longer such a "virtuous cycle" can prevail.

That's what assessing risk is all about. When you see a confluence of events, good or bad, you have to ask two questions. The first is "How long can this continue?" and the second is, to borrow from Cole Porter, "Is it the good turtle soup or merely the mock?" When you are seeking opportunity, you are attempting to make sense out of uncertainty, to make comprehensible the bits of information you have that don't seem to fit into a pattern. In the intelligence business, there is a saying that before you can connect the dots, you have to know what a dot is. Not all information will fit into an investment thesis, and sometimes, no matter what you do, you won't be able to make sense of what you are looking at.

That was before Google. One of the tricks I use is to take two or three words and type them together into Google and see what comes up, and then take another two or three related to the same subject, and then begin trying various combinations. What happens is fascinating. Let's take *Lula, economic reform,* and *China,* put them into the Google window, and hit the SEARCH button. As early as February 2003, right after Lula took office, evidence began to turn up on the Web that he was going to attempt to move Brazil down the path of economic reform at the same time that he was going to court China. By October of that year, the two nations had already signed the first of a series of trade agreements. Since China's economy was growing fiercely and Lula was not about to do anything stupid with Brazil's economy, there were already enough signals emerging that Brazil might be a good bet. But back in 1994, long before Lula's arrival, the U.S. Department of Commerce conducted a study that identified Brazil as a "big emerging market," a nation that, if it could get its economic and fiscal house in order, had the potential to become a major trading partner with the United States. In other words, the signs that the Brazilian economy was, as Soros put it, "a waterfall you could put your bucket under" began to emerge more than a decade ago. The most opportunistic investors might have jumped in and invested then and been burned by a major currency crisis in 1998 and 1999, which was caused, ironically, by too much foreign investment (in the year before Brazil's monetary meltdown, foreign currency inflows, chasing inflation-fueled interest rates, jumped 140 percent). Naturally, global investors who had been burned in the currency crisis were intensely skeptical that Brazil would get its economic house in order when Lula took over in 2002, especially since he had run on a fairly left-wing platform, which always gives capitalist investors in the West the heebie-jeebies, so little capital flowed back in as the Brazilian economy began to recover. But a handful of smart investors spotted a strong opportunity here, a waterfall, and placed their buckets appropriately. All through 2003, 2004, and 2005, you could have made handsome returns by investing in Brazil, until the Bovespa took a break in late June 2006. As it turned out, Brazil was the real turtle soup.

Which brings us back to the first question: how long can this continue? Ask yourself this question: what has changed since the Brazilian economy took off? Inflation is down, not up. Interest rates continue to drop. The nation's foreign exchange reserves, now at $57 billion, appear to signal a healthy economy. Brazil has paid off its $15 billion debt to the International Monetary Fund, and commodity prices remain strong. Coffee is up so much that Starbucks has had to raise its prices. Brazil's investment in sugar cane for ethanol has put a floor under formerly sagging sugar prices, and it is now the largest meat producer in the world. That's the upside of Brazil. The downside is that Lula's government has been plagued by charges of corruption, which led to the resignation of his finance minister. Party discipline is breaking down, as Brazil's poor, who have not benefited nearly as much from economic reform as promised, are growing restive. Worst of all, there is simply too much foreign portfolio investment, at least $100 billion, almost twice as much as a year earlier. Whenever there's too much money on one side of an investment and not enough on the other, there is a stronger than even chance that the investment's value will fall. It is a simple illustration of supply and demand.

Too many sellers will emerge at the first sign of trouble, and not nearly enough buyers.

What is true for developing nations such as Brazil is equally true for developed nations like the United States. For a long time, Americans watched interest rate changes by the Federal Reserve and bet on the general direction of stocks and bonds from there. When interest rates began to rise, stocks generally would fall, and vice versa. But the U.S. economy has become more interwoven with the global economy, so it is harder to discern the circumstances that will combine to push or pull the equity markets. That has caused investors to be flooded with information, which leads to overload, which can lead to indecision. How do you cope with too much information? Make yourself a balance sheet that contains four categories: *politics, economics, the environment,* and *exogenous factors.*

POLITICS

Political factors, for instance, might include the willingness of an administration to rein in spending. The current Bush administration has shown no such discipline, and in fact, because Republicans dominated both the executive branch and Congress for most of the past few years, there was no counterforce to keep them from passing whatever tax-cutting or deficit-enlarging legislation they wanted. If Democrats had been in power, the situation would have been exactly the same. Now that a counterbalance between the White House and Congress has been restored, the tendency by the party in power to run amok to the detriment of taxpayers and consumers may be dampened.

Other political factors include *how* the party in control of the White House exercises power. Are they imperious, or are they relatively open? Again, this is not a Republican versus Democrat issue. Each side has behaved badly when it had the reins of power, and it is discouraging to investors whenever that happens. Both sides have attempted at one time or another to force the Fed to make decisions about interest rates motivated by politics, which is always to the detriment of investor decision making.

ECONOMICS

Is GDP growing at a good clip? Are corporate profits rising or falling? What about job creation, consumer debt levels, and consumer savings? How is the housing market doing? All these are economic influences on your decision making. So, too, are trade balances, foreign exchange reserves, the money supply, and the cost of energy.

THE ENVIRONMENT

By environmental factors, I don't mean the physical environment literally, although that can come into play if a natural disaster causes a lot of destruction. Aside from the property losses, such disasters can suck resources from one part of the country to another and create imbalances that can stress the economy. That's why GDP dropped half a point after Hurricane Katrina. But other "environmental" factors are the quantitative versus qualitative data and the mood of the nation. Consumer confidence is an environmental measure, not an economic one, because it is an attempt to measure the zeitgeist of the country, not the true state of economic well-being. Presidential popularity is another environmental factor. When it is low, as it has been for the last couple of years, ordinary people are uncertain about how well their nation will be led when crisis erupts. And as we know, when people are uncertain, they don't invest.

EXOGENOUS FACTORS

Finally, exogenous factors are that portion of the chart labeled *visible yet incomprehensible.* They are factors or bits of information we see but don't know how to evaluate. If they are large enough, we can make some guesses. When severe acute respiratory syndrome (SARS) burst on the world scene in February 2003, no one knew if it was going to be a small but containable disease or a global pandemic. By the time the last death was reported two months later, much of Asia's economic life had shut down, and the region's GDP growth had lost half a percentage point for six months. The repeated warnings by the World Health Organization that avian flu might have even more dire consequences makes that one of those exogenous events that you have to account for when you are considering your risk profile. Here's another: when Indonesia was hit by a destructive tsunami in December 2004, that nation's stock market went down but a blip. Why? While the world was shocked by the huge loss of life in Indonesia, the Indonesians weren't. They have been hit by epic natural disasters for generations and are somewhat fatalistic about such events when they happen. Much more worrisome for investors, though, is the tsunami's aftermath. Banda Aceh, the province most affected by the destruction, has veered sharply to the religious right and has adopted *sharia*, Islamic law, which is very conservative, especially regarding the treatment of women. Indonesia is the largest Islamic nation in the world, and should the rest of the state follow Banda Aceh, that development would not be good for investors in Indonesia's booming economy.

Okay. Let's quickly review. First, whether you are investing in the developing world or the developed, you need good information, acquired early, to determine whether or not you should even consider making an investment. Second, you need to be able to assess how long the confluence of events that you have spotted is likely to exist. The longer it does, the greater the chances that if you get in relatively early, you will do extremely well, and that if you get in a bit later, there will still be enough time for you to earn a decent return. Third, you have to determine whether what you are seeing is a real change in direction or merely the appearance of one, a mirage that could evaporate in an instant, along with your investment. Do those things, and you can begin to answer the *developed versus developing* binary.

CHAPTER 2

THE RULE *versus* THE RULE OF POWER OF LAW

Having just spent some time looking at the developed world versus the developing world, I'd like to look at a different facet of that binary: the rule of power versus the rule of law. Looking at these two is meant to answer the following question: can I invest safely in a country where the deck is seemingly stacked against me? In nations such as Russia, China, Egypt, Saudi Arabia, and Indonesia, as well as many other emerging markets, the rule of law is weak and the rule of individual power is strong. As my friend Ian Bremmer, president of the Eurasia Group, a New York–based international relations consultancy, once described Russia, "Putin is a strong president, but there is no strong presidency in Russia." In other words, the rule of law is weak and altogether too much power is concentrated in the handful of people with whom Putin surrounds himself. In the old Soviet Union, when the Communist Party was the dominant institution, the nation was a kleptocracy, a state where officials used their power to steal from the citizens. Russia today has exhibited many of those same traits, particularly with the confiscation of Yukos Oil, the jailing of the company's president, and the assassination of opposition political figures and journalists.

I do not mean to pick on Russia. It is just one example of a nation that still suffers from weak laws when it comes to protecting property rights and investments. Even when laws appear strong, the judicial systems behind them may be too weak or arbitrary to guarantee that an investor's rights will be upheld in a dispute. Some nations even make distinctions between local shareholders and foreign holders when it comes to rights, so that a foreign investor could wind up at the end of the line in a claims dispute. How can a country where such behavior exists still attract investment?

It goes back to the question of how you assess risk and the direction of reform. Let's go back to Russia for a moment. There are many astute investors who believe that Russia, after seventy-five years under Communist rule, has nowhere to go but up. It is rich in energy, and because of its geography, Russia has the ability to become an effective bridge between Europe and Asia. But except for a period of less than a decade before World War I, Russia has had no experience with the rule of law, and it is struggling to define its legal system. President Putin takes strong umbrage at the idea that he is backsliding toward a Soviet-style government ruled in secret by a small handful of meretricious people, and he points to falling inflation, a strengthening currency, and rising wages as proof that he is going in the right direction. That has yet to be proved conclusively, and Russia's strong showing has been offset by rising AIDS, a shrinking population beset by alcoholism, aging, and worker absenteeism, and chronic violence and drug use among its youth. Also, thanks to Russia's far northern climate, the energy inputs required for everything from heating apartments to exploring for energy are far higher than for any other developed or developing nation, which puts Russia at a substantial disadvantage on world markets. Given the long tradition in Russia of distrusting the common man, the nation gives the appearance of reverting to its old Soviet model, even if it is not.

Despite rising investor doubts and a chorus of criticism of its behavior regarding the seizure of Yukos, the July 2006 initial public offering in London of Rosneft, a Russian oil company, raised some $15 billion, proving that certain foreign investors were willing to take a chance on Russia. Overwhelmingly, these investors were large energy companies looking to cement ties with Rosneft so that they might gain a future share of Russia's oil. Individual investors and even institutional investors were notably absent. Why? The political risks were simply too great for most.

So does this mean that when you see a nation with investing potential but weak rule of law, you should stay away? Not necessarily. There are two things that you have to know about investing when the rule of law is weak. The first is that if you see a market about which you are pessimistic rising, *open your mind* to find the reason. The second is that once you find the reason, start looking for a mechanism that allows you to invest with some prospect of getting your money out.

What do I mean by "open your mind" in this case? Don't reject a market simply because you don't like the politics or the players or the country or its philosophy. If you are willing to do a little digging, you will generally find a sound reason why a market is rising. (You might still balk at investing for moral reasons, perhaps not investing in the Sudan because of the killings in Darfur. But that doesn't mean that other investors will be as squeamish. Where there is opportunity, somebody will take it.) For example, the post-9/11 crash of U.S. securities convinced people in many emerging markets that they needed to do something with their money besides park it in the United States. Many of them began looking at their own home markets and discovered that politics or the local economy had changed or that they were able to import back to their home states not only their capital but also knowledge and connections that they had acquired in their own years abroad. Smart Russians, Brazilians, Mexicans, Saudis, Kuwaitis, Egyptians, and citizens of many other countries began bringing their money home and, because of family connections and local knowledge, started to invest their money in rising industries, entrepreneurial ventures, and real estate. Between 2000 and 2002, this flood of repatriated capital became the foundation for much of the subsequent emerging-market boom that leveled off in mid-2006. Much of that boom took place in nations that were advancing along the path of reform, but some of the hottest markets were in nations like Saudi Arabia and Kuwait, where social and political reform have until recently been unthinkable. What made those markets hot was that the people who were repatriating their capital knew something you didn't. Their local knowledge gave them the confidence to invest, and because they were part of the inner circle, they had a reasonable expectation that *they* would be treated fairly.

Your job is to take advantage of that change in market dynamics by finding someone who will make it *his* mission to figure out how to lay off part of the risk that you see in order to attract *your* money, as your money entering his market will cause it to rise at an even faster rate. In the case of many emerging markets, this means country-based mutual funds or exchange-traded funds. In country-based mutual funds, the fund manager has made some sort of arrangement with the national stock market and local securities commission so that foreign capital can be invested and held in the country. Many of these funds, especially in emerging markets, maintain a high degree of liquidity and have holding periods, in which only a small percentage of the stock that the fund owns can be redeemed at any point in time. These mechanisms prevent capital flight in case things go wrong with the country's economy. National securities commissions reason that if foreign investors are going to profit from gains in their economy, they ought to share some of the pain when the economy does not do as well. At the same time, they want some insurance against unexpected capital flight if there is too large a buildup of foreign investment through a particular fund.

If all this seems like a lot of trouble, it is because Americans have been conditioned by more than seventy years of securities law and enforcement to believe that they can get a reasonably fair shake when they invest. We have a long history of legal intervention in the stock markets, going back to the Great Depression, which followed the first great period of popular stock ownership in the United States. When stock market manipulation wiped out many investors in the late 1920s, the U.S. government stepped in and formed the Securities and Exchange Commission, whose primary responsibility was to create fairness in the marketplace. Since then, the SEC has written many new rules, yet from time to time there are scandals that shake the faith of investors in American markets. In addition to the SEC, other bodies, such as the Financial and Accounting Standards (FASB) Board, have emerged to write rules about corporate behavior and accounting transparency, yet periodically companies will push the envelope on rules and suddenly find themselves the subject of a Justice Department investigation or even, occasionally, the subject of prosecution. This goes both for companies that issue shares and for the brokerages and financial institutions that buy and sell them.

American adherence to the rule of law may seem cumbersome. But just as physical standards are necessary to ensure that you are getting both the quality and the quantity you pay for—the origin of uniform weights and measures more than five thousand years ago in early historic India is considered the foundation of modern civilization, because it allowed different cultures to trade goods according to a standardized and agreed-upon system, and the substitution of money for physical goods occurred not long after that—legal and accounting standards are equally necessary to ensure that when you buy a security or make an investment, you also get what you paid for. The representations that a company or municipal authority makes when it issues securities are supposed to disclose fully all risks so that you can make a comparative evaluation of all the choices available to you as an investor. If a company or other issuer doesn't do that, it's like tilting the machine in pinball. You might win for a while, but invariably, the machine will eventually cancel your game. If a company lures in investors with false information, as, for example, Enron did, its stock may prosper for a time, but eventually, the investors are going to get burned.

As Americans have invested abroad and as foreigners have gained experience in investing in the United States, the American system of financial transparency has spread abroad. Some emerging-market nations, such as India, where investors were burned by repeated stock market settlement scandals in the late 1980s, have installed investment settlement and monitoring software on electronic exchanges that is now equal or superior to any system in the United States. Other nations and regions, such as the European Union, have substantially beefed up their accounting and disclosure laws after investors were rocked by accounting scandals involving companies such as the Italian dairy giant Parmalat, the Dutch supermarket company Ahold, and the Belgian supermarket company Food Lion, among others.

This brings us to another one of those aspects of decision making that you must embrace: if an investment sounds too good to be true, it almost always is. When you are evaluating an investment opportunity, figure out whether the reward and the risk are commensurate. If someone tells you that you can get a 15 percent return with little or no risk of losing your money, can that be believed? Well, as we have seen in the past few years, it has been true for a number of emerging markets. But that is because of a confluence of events that may not repeat for a generation—or may come again within a few months. The investing landscape constantly shifts, and you have to learn how to read it. What appears to be a waterfall right now might dry up in just a few months or a few years, so you have to watch the flow into the bucket as well as the future of the waterfall above. Move on before the flow turns into a trickle or dries up altogether.

A nation might look as if it is under the rule of law and yet not be. When you are making an investment, you are investing in the future potential of a company, an industry, and even a nation, and having that potential be thwarted by the law is as bad as having it thwarted by a powerful dictator or coterie of leaders. In order for a company or a nation to grow, there must always be room for competition. So when France will not allow an American company to take over a French firm, that is as bad for investors as China's poorly defined shareholder laws, which make direct investment there such a risky proposition, or, for that matter, as when American political considerations get in the way of, say, a Chinese takeover of a U.S. oil company. When Latin American nations pass "national patrimony" laws that protect certain segments of the economy, they discourage capital investment. Not only do they deny investors the opportunity to make money, but worse, they often condemn a nation like Mexico, which protects its oil industry, to do without desperately needed development. Whenever you read about a nation blocking competition, it is, at the very least, a cautionary flag that should make you think twice before you invest.

Let's review. First, keep an open mind when you invest. Just because you don't like a country's politics or a company's business doesn't mean you can't earn a good return on an investment. I'm not opposed to social investing: if you really hate the tobacco companies, by all means don't invest in them. If you think that Saudi Arabia is a dangerous place, by all means put your money someplace else. But if you are going for the best returns year in and year out, you are going to find that ethics is a one-way street lined with money. Don't ever invest in anything illegal, but otherwise, learn to look at all opportunities neutrally and equally, with a mixture of knowledge, skepticism, and a healthy worldview.

Second, learn to lay off risk. If an investment is risky, there is always some iteration of it that can be created that has a lower return but far less risk, such as investing in a basket of equities with an option on the national currency, so that if the currency rises and the basket stagnates, you can still come out ahead, or if the basket rises and the currency stagnates, you get the same result. Your job is to find that proper combination of risk and reward that makes you comfortable, that does not put your capital in jeopardy, and that ensures that you will get a good payoff on the upside and leave you minimally harmed if things go wrong. I am a strong believer in protection. When you go to Las Vegas to play blackjack, the house offers you "insurance" whenever the dealer has an ace showing. If you would insure your bet at the gambling table, why would you possibly go, as the Asians put it, "naked long," which is their expression for what we call "buy and hold"? If you forgo a little of the upside, there is a much greater chance that you will come away with enough to make your forays abroad worthwhile.

The third takeaway is "Follow the money." You can't possibly be an expert on every opportunity, but somewhere there is an expert of some kind, so learn to follow monetary flows. If you see a market begin to rise, find out why. Newspapers, the Internet, and scholarly journals will provide you with more than enough information to help you decide whether a potential investment has legs. If it does, put your bucket under it.

Finally, not all decision making is about following the moment; sometimes it's about seeing developing trends. You don't want to waste your time with ideas and investments that will fall apart after a couple of weeks. You want to be in long enough to get a solid return without having to spend so much time micromanaging your decision that you worry yourself sick. Remember, your own time is valuable.

CHAPTER 3

COPYRIGHTS *versus* COPYING

In a digital world where intellectual property is ever more valuable and, paradoxically, more copyable, copyrights, like patent walls and other forms of protectionism, aren't what they used to be. Where in the past an upstart company would turn its engineering talent loose on improving a product in order to break down a patent wall, now companies simply copy the product, slap on a phony label, and sell it in competition with bona fide goods. In 2005, according to the Organization for Economic Cooperation and Development (OECD), counterfeiting cost legitimate manufacturers more than $600 billion and developed nations about a quarter of a million jobs and several billion dollars in tax revenues. But the same is true in emerging nations. Russia reports that the flood of counterfeit goods entering that country costs the government more than $1 billion a year in tax receipts, which is a staggering amount, considering that Russia's total GDP is only slightly more than $800 billion, with the government taking in perhaps $100 billion in taxes.

Who are the culprits? It is easy to blame China, where so much manufacturing takes place, but counterfeiting has become a worldwide epidemic in a rising market of several billion new consumers. I am not condoning counterfeiting when I say that, but I am recognizing that demand can create opportunities for supply. While many companies rightly complain that they are being ripped off by counterfeiters, many more companies willfully or stupidly allow themselves to be taken advantage of. There is a longstanding practice that exists in many industries, especially the garment industry, where knocking off someone else's designs is endemic, that consists of lowering the per-unit cost of goods by extending a mill run and then selling the extras either at a discount or to a jobber, who will off-load goods to small stores and even flea markets. Look at all the "company discount stores" that Americans flock to in search of bargains. At one time those stores used to sell "seconds," goods with a slight flaw or that were last season's merchandise. Now they often sell end-of-run firsts, at a slight discount from their mall stores, and reap higher profits. The Chinese, who manufacture an increasing share of America's goods, merely do the same thing, extending a run of, say, golf clubs, and selling—illegally—the extras out the back door, lowering their overall manufacturing costs while not passing on their savings to the manufacturer with whom they contract to make the clubs. Is the manufacturer hurt? Sometimes, if the counterfeit goods make it into the manufacturer's primary markets, a firm will be hurt. But often, the goods are going into markets where they are otherwise unaffordable and, often, where the company does not have much of a marketing presence.

Increasingly, the real cost to manufacturers comes when consumers buy knockoffs of branded products and those products fail, causing the consumer to sue or to stop using the company's products. This places the manufacturer in a bind, because often, it is less expensive for a manufacturer to replace a knockoff with real goods than to go through the hassle of a lawsuit. As a result, companies spend hundreds of millions of dollars a year policing their brands and replacing counterfeit goods with real ones, money that comes off the bottom line and ultimately hurts shareholders.

Investors want assurances that their company's fortunes won't be adversely affected by copying, while consumers just want cheap goods. How do you choose companies that can protect themselves against copying in a world where, as time goes on, what's yours is mine—and vice versa?

The answer depends upon the size of the company, the size of the crime, and where it takes place. If a company is small and the amount of counterfeiting is large in relation to its sales, that's like being shot with a large-caliber pistol. The counterfeiting could do damage sufficient to put the company out of business, though location is also a factor. If you get shot in front of a hospital, chances are you will survive if you get to the emergency room quickly, but if you are attacked in a neighborhood far from home, you are likely to become a statistic. The same goes for counterfeiting. Much of that $600 billion in injury the OECD claims is notional, which is to say that it represents lost opportunity rather than lost sales. But what if your product is too expensive to buy in the country where it is counterfeited and consumers can only afford to purchase the knockoff? Is that a real lost sale or a notional one? I'm not a lawyer, and it's not a position I'd choose to defend, but from an investing perspective, I can say with some authority that if most of the knockoffs of a well-known brand are sold in markets where the company does not now have large sales, the opportunity cost might be large, but the real cost is small. If you are investing in a large company with sales overwhelmingly concentrated in a few large developed markets, those companies face a smaller threat from counterfeiters. If your investment is in a smaller company, counterfeiting could have a significant impact on the bottom line.

Whether you are a manufacturer or an investor, another way to ask the question is, what exactly is it that you want to protect, and what can be protected? Apple thought it had the answer to copy protection when it developed the iPod by differentiating its software from that of other audio players using the MP3 format and by making file sharing impossible by making file transfers unidirectional, so that you could transfer songs or other media to and from your own iPod but not to and from someone else's iPod. This technology has reaped Apple Computer a fortune and driven up the price of its shares. Apple will sell billions of songs and hundreds of millions of iPods and iPhones.

But that protection may prove short-lived. The French government, pandering to its young people after a series of student uprisings in the spring of 2006, has attempted to force Apple to make its file-sharing system compatible with other MP3 players, which is tantamount to taking away Apple's only real competitive advantage. The European Union has jumped into the fray on the side of the French, again in the name of competition, even though there are no European-made MP3 players of any significance on the market.

What does this mean for investors? Probably little, at this point. But if nations decide for political purposes that they want to break up a company's strong position in order to pander to local politics, it defeats the entire purpose of investing, which is to earn a solid return from the efforts of the best companies. What should you do in those circumstances? Watch the company and see how it reacts. A company like Apple can litigate its way out of trouble, and Apple CEO Steve Jobs has not been afraid to take on the French, but more important, Apple continues to innovate.

Remember, when you invest, you are making a bet on the future, not on the present. In fact, whenever you make a decision, your choices are as much about the future as they are about the here and now. The decision to buy a home, for example, is not just about how much you like the house you just saw and its current value on the real estate market. It is equally, perhaps even more so, about the community in which you choose to live, the commute you are going to have to make to your job, the real estate taxes you are likely to pay in the future, and the future value of your real estate versus that of the town next door. All of those considerations and more, such as the quality of the schools, the safety of the neighborhood, the quality of the shopping, and a dozen other little things, all go into the decision to buy one house over another.

It's the same with a stock or bond, and one of the decisions you have to make is how vulnerable the company is to competition, both legal and illegal. Does your company have a long and successful history of beating back copyright or patent infringement, as does, say, the Walt Disney Company? At the same time, does it also have a long history of innovation, such as 3M does? Most American companies are spending less and less each year on research and development, preferring to buy new products in the marketplace rather than invest in creating their own. Recently Procter & Gamble has become extremely adept at acquiring new products that are then placed under an existing P&G brand banner, such as Crest's new whitening toothbrush, which was invented by outside parties. Through P&G's "connect and develop" program, along with improvements in other aspects of innovation related to product cost, design, and marketing, the company's R&D productivity has, according to the company, increased by nearly 60 percent. The innovation success rate has more than doubled, while the cost of innovation has fallen. R&D investment as a percentage of sales is down from 4.8 percent in 2000 to 3.4 percent today. And, in the last two years, P&G has launched more than 100 new products for which some aspect of execution came from outside the company.

P&G has presented this notion of connecting with the world's inventors as a new paradigm for boosting profits. Perhaps it is. There are millions of talented engineers, scientists, and inventors around the world who can add vastly more to a company's talent pool than its own limited R&D staff, no matter the company's size. Moreover, as new markets emerge, there will be enormous numbers of new engineers designing products and services for the billions of emerging consumers in search of the same creature comforts, or some variation of them, that Americans now enjoy.

But there are perils in an open-architecture system of innovation. What one person invents, another can easily copy, and long before a large company can put its patent wall of protection around an outside invention, copies of it may turn up in the market stalls of Shanghai or Mumbai or on the streets of New York or Los Angeles. In one sense, this takes nothing away from the company that purchased the invention or technology, since the potential market was infinite before the product made it to the shelves, and no company ever gets 100 percent of any market. But in another sense it hurts the company, and it hurts investors as well, because if an open-sourced product attracts one copycat, it will attract many copycats, especially if it is popular. At some point, that theft will affect sales.

Another way for a company to protect itself is through brand management and through innovation in packaging. There were MP3 players on the market for several years before Apple launched the iPod in late 2001, yet within a year, Apple had dominated the market. Part of it was the firm agreement that Apple struck with nearly all the record companies so that it could offer millions of songs. But just as important, the iPod's packaging, elegant design, simplicity of use, and elegant human touches made it a winner. In an era when companies are increasingly outsourcing their innovation, sound brand management commensurately hinges on how well the product is presented to the public.

A quick review: First, copyrights and patents aren't what they used to be. In a world where even innovation is outsourced, a company might be more robust—and a better investment—because it has wider access to a greater number of talented people, but it also means that the company must be relentless in innovating lest it be nibbled to death by ducks. If the company in which you have invested isn't thoroughly committed to its own future, through the protection of its brands, its patents, and its capability to innovate, why should you be?

Second, innovation takes many forms. Technology is one of them, but so is what the product looks like, how it is sold, how it is serviced, and how well the company stands behind it. The genius of Steve Jobs is not just that he is selling beautiful machinery; it is also that his stores are an enjoyable experience and that Apple's repair by replacement encourages consumers to purchase the warranty, because they know that Apple is still providing them with consumer protection. As an investor, you can be certain that companies that look out for their customers also look out for their shareholders.

Third, emerging markets—in fact, all markets—belong to those willing to commit to them. A company that does not realize that small-budget consumers cannot afford their goods and does not make allowances by finding new ways to make them affordable presents an open invitation to anyone who can. Think Apple versus Louis Vuitton. Apple fights competitors, while Vuitton fights knockoffs. Those who counterfeit will always find a ready market as long as companies are less than flexible about opening their own markets instead of having someone else do it for them. When you are thinking about investing in a company, spend some time on its website in the product sales and marketing area and take a look at how they are working to open new markets. If you see innovation at work, the company is probably innovating in other key areas as well.

CHAPTER 4

ANTI-IMMIGRATION *versus* MIGRATION OF TALENT

The United States built its wealth on the hard work of millions of immigrants and on the talents of people who could not obtain an education in their own countries. Once here, these people were able to develop, to society's benefit and to their own benefit. As a nation, the United States is still relatively open to immigrants, although the demographic character of our immigrant pool is changing. Part of the problem we face with immigrants is that while the nature of immigration has changed little—it is still the poor, the opportunity-seeking, the person looking for a new start—the nation to which they are coming has changed dramatically.

Between 1620 and about 1950, immigrants, mainly from Europe, were arriving at a place not much different from where they had left. There were fewer people and land was cheaper, but for the most part, those arriving were usually better educated than those who were here, and often, they came with a little money, which enabled many of them to open businesses soon after they landed. Following World War II, though, the balance began to shift remarkably. The United States was expanding its education system, while Europe and Asia were not, and the United States was on its way to becoming the most technologically advanced and prosperous nation on the planet while Europe and Asia struggled to rebuild after the war. From 1950 on, the gap has continued to widen between the United States and many parts of the world, especially Asia, Latin America, and Africa. Immigrants from those regions are often bewildered by what they find in the United States, and they sometimes represent a liability to the nation since they bring little with them in the way of marketable skills. This shift is the crux of the modern debate about immigration, and it has made many Americans leery about keeping our doors open.

In Europe, the problem is more basic. European nations that have long prided themselves on their liberal governments and social benefits systems have been overrun by millions of poor Asians and Africans. Most of those immigrants are Muslims, and they bring with them a religious and cultural perspective that often appears unbridgeable. Europe's nations have chosen to deal with the Muslim incursion in as many ways as there are countries in the European Union: The French insist that anyone living on their soil act as if they are French, and so have enacted a series of bills forcing social conformity. The Dutch, meanwhile, have allowed their Muslim community to maintain its own customs and even to establish its own schools. The responses from other European nations fall somewhere along that spectrum, but none can be said to have found a solution. Meanwhile, Japan has spent billions of dollars on robotics research for devices that will perform the labor that would ordinarily be performed by low-wage immigrants rather than allow foreigners to live among them.

While national responses to immigration raise acute social and racial questions, which we'll leave to the sociologists and politicians, the more important question for me is, what role, if any, does immigration play in creating investment opportunity? There have been many studies in the United States that purport to show that immigrants—legal and otherwise—generate more in income and taxes than they consume in social services. But dollars and cents often come up against sense and sensibility, and integrating new groups is often problematic from a social and cultural perspective.

The immigration argument takes on a different tone when you are investing in a company. You are ultimately investing in people, and a company's ability to attract "the best and the brightest" from around the world is a large part of what the management consultants McKinsey & Company call the "global war for talent." It is a war whose outcome is increasingly in dispute. It used to be that the best scientists and engineers came to U.S. companies to work, while their less talented counterparts back home were relegated to back-office work or updating legacy computer codes. Despite the huge numbers of engineers that pour out of Chinese and Indian technical universities, historically only a handful have that extra spark of genius that produces world-beating competitive products. Now, with capital readily available in their own countries, the most talented are beginning to stay home to launch their own locally centered, highly competitive enterprises. Companies such as India's Infosys or China's Lenovo have made immigration an investment issue by their ability to keep the best local talent happy at home and off the visa lines.

American companies have tried to take advantage of this phenomenon by outsourcing much of their production, design, and now, even marketing (McDonald's current domestic urban-oriented "I'm lovin' it" campaign had its origins at an advertising agency in Germany), but, as I noted earlier, that migration of enterprise creates its own problems (see Chapter 3). The shift of technological prowess from one nation to another is not a new story: the American textile industry of the late eighteenth century was built on power-loom designs stolen by Samuel Slater from British mills and reconstructed in the United States. But few nations have intentionally sent their technology abroad with the kind of intensity that the United States has since the beginning of the 1990s. We educate the smartest foreigners in our universities, allow them to work unimpeded, and then finance their enterprises when they return home.

While there is no real method to this apparent madness, there are results. Start-up enterprises abroad purchase a vast number of American technology licenses, more than $5 billion worth annually. These licenses are often accompanied by the purchases of specialized machinery. Indeed, the United States continues to dominate the world trade in high-technology goods, producing intellectual property with a value of more than $5 trillion over the past twenty years. Though about $56 billion of that is lost through counterfeiting, the rate at which U.S. companies continue to produce products of ever higher value should comfort investors and politicians alike.

More important to this discussion, though, is the value of immigrants as a market that stimulates both general economic development and the creation of new intellectual property. Today's immigrants have both wider and different needs from the immigrants of old. They want products that conform more to their preestablished way of life, culture, and language, which means that companies have to come up with both new products and new ways to market them. One might argue that this is inefficient, since it threatens the economies of scale and productivity on which large companies' profits depend, but in fact, companies that take the time to develop strategies and products specific to new markets do very well indeed; consider the *Miami Herald*'s decision to produce a distinct Spanish-language newspaper for the third of Miamians who prefer their news in Spanish. By spending the time to create products desirable to immigrants on their own terms, companies also wind up creating products and services that find ready markets in the home nations from which those immigrants spring. Indeed, a study by worldwide consulting firm Deloitte Touche Tohmatsu shows that companies often make few changes in the products and services they sell to consumers in the home countries of immigrants.

Perhaps more important, the effect of immigration on investment is to create opportunity in the form of new businesses. While large companies increasingly recognize the value of immigrants to their bottom line as customers who typically spend more on products than their better-established native counterparts, many immigrants also recognize the value of going into business for themselves. Despite the belief that immigrants don't contribute much to society besides low-level work, they are in fact instrumental in starting businesses that serve other immigrants. In the United States, individuals start more than 550,000 new businesses a month, according to the Ewing Marion Kauffman Foundation. Latin American immigrants start more business than any other group, followed by immigrants in general. While the vast majority of these businesses either fail or remain small, increasing numbers of them become larger enterprises, and some of them become businesses that go public and represent dynamic investment opportunities, such as Goya Foods and the Miami-based Sterling Financial Group of Companies. Also, increasing numbers of these businesses are in high-technology sectors of industry, especially communications, because in a world of instant global communications, immigrants increasingly maintain cultural ties to their home countries.

Immigrants also represent another kind of opportunity. As noted earlier, they often return home, taking with them their knowledge. This is not only technical knowledge but also cultural knowledge of things American, which makes them natural consumers of U.S. goods when they return home as well as distributors and cultural ambassadors of those goods. Go into any large Asian city and look at the proliferation of American fast-food chains, and you are looking at Asian Americans who have returned home and brought with them franchise agreements to open these stores. These returned immigrants take with them not just a nostalgia for the developed world they have just left but also the ability to upgrade their own countries with the knowledge they now carry. Nations such as China and Vietnam would never have developed as rapidly as they did were it not for the large numbers of their citizens who had worked in the United States for a number of years and then returned home with expertise that their countrymen could not gather working domestically. While many oppose this kind of globalization, arguing that the jobs and skills that immigrants bring back to their nations do as much harm as good, the jobs they generate and the investment capital they attract is beyond dispute.

Finally, the great value of immigration is that it creates synthesis. Americans now consume more salsa than ketchup. This is partly because as domestic palates age, taste buds are lost. But if there had not been a large influx of Mexicans beginning in the 1970s, there would be no salsa to perk up American taste buds. Immigrants have given us a world of cuisines from which to choose, and those cuisines have been at the heart of restaurant investment options, from Chi-Chi's to P.F. Changs to several large pizza companies. While none has done as well as all-American McDonald's, without the movement of migrants around the world, it is doubtful whether chains such as McDonald's, Burger King, and now Starbucks could expand so easily abroad. Starbucks now has more than three thousand stores in thirty-four countries and expects to reach twenty thousand international outlets someday. Their ability to stimulate coffee demand has already benefited Brazil and the price of coffee beans, but it has also generated tens of thousands of jobs. There is, in fact, a remarkable synergy between immigration and the movement of American businesses around the world, especially those that have a franchising base.

What is needed is not less immigration and movement of people, but more. It would be good for this nation's investors if more Americans would learn a foreign language and take the leap to work abroad for a couple of years. The new cultural knowledge and the skills they would acquire, not to mention the expanded worldview—that *Weltanschauung* again—would be of great benefit in helping the United States maintain its competitive posture. The more we know about them, the more things we can sell them. Moreover, aside from the social and sometimes economic strains, the United States could probably use a little more immigration, not less. The native-born population continues to drop because of delayed marriages, divorce, smaller families, and what the Nobel Prize–winning physiologist Sir Peter Medawar once called "the ability of fecundity and longevity to overtake fertility" as incomes rise, a phenomenon now taking place in nearly every nation on the planet. It is only continued immigration, both legal and otherwise, that adds incremental sales to large discount retailers such as Wal-Mart.

Let's review. On the whole, immigration is good for investors. It brings new customers, new incentives to innovate, new markets, new competitors, and new capital into the market. The savings rates of immigrants are higher than those of the native born, which adds to capital formation. What immigrants, legal or otherwise, take out of the system in terms of municipal services, they probably make up in direct taxes and certainly make up in sales taxes on the goods they purchase. Immigrants start more new businesses—and therefore are a greater source of new employment—than their native-born counterparts. Additionally, these new companies add to the capital stock of the community in another way. They bring their talents, hopes, dreams, and skills to countries that are increasingly postindustrial and therefore less inclined to do the jobs that only those at the bottom rungs of the economic ladder are willing to take on. All in all, there are few reasons to oppose immigration from an investment perspective, much less a cultural one.

CHAPTER 5

TOKYO *versus* SHANGHAI

Or France versus Spain.

Or Milan versus Dublin.

Or New York versus Paris.

In real estate, the secret to success is always "location, location, location." It's also true in financial markets. Some cities and countries offer more robust investment opportunities than others.

In *The Rise of the Creative Class*, Professor Richard Florida argued that cities and nations that foster creativity are better places to invest than those that do not. By Florida's definitions, places like Shanghai, Spain, Dubai, and Dublin, which are all vibrant, bustling economies, are great places for investment, while Tokyo, Paris, Milan, and parts of the United States are not.

Is Florida right? Once again, it depends upon what you are looking for in an investment. The blossoming group of cities and countries listed above, and others like them, have had over the decades (recent dips not withstanding) hot real estate markets, relatively easy access to capital, lots of entrepreneurial talent, and an almost festive atmosphere that I call the four F's—food, fashion, film, and fun. If a city or country has all of those in abundance, it likely has a very robust economy. (Neither Florida nor I is the first to say this: a century ago, when Paris was a more vibrant city, Marcel Proust wrote that his city floated along on good food, interesting sex, and intelligent conversation.) And robust economies generate investment opportunities.

At least, so the theory goes. But it's not that simple.

The money to float a rising economy has to come from somewhere, and that usually means imported capital. It isn't the smart city fathers who one day decide that a city should grow. Sometimes there is a single benefactor, or a government agency will issue bonds to build up local infrastructure, or a legislature will grant tax breaks to companies that come into an area. But none of those, by themselves or in combination, will turn a moribund area hot. For that to happen, it usually takes a distant investor who observes a city or country, makes a visit or two, is impressed with what he sees, and evangelizes the new area to his investor friends. Those investors swoop in, buy up real estate on the cheap, and either fix it up or develop it, usually hiring a couple of world-class architects to bring their own flair (and media attention) along. Quicker than you can say "Santiago Calatrava," your city is suddenly on everyone's lips, and real estate values begin to take off. That enables the first round of owners to cash in, and if they also own businesses, they can use the capital to expand. But often, they don't have to, because once a city becomes hot, it attracts other kinds of risk capital as well. Suddenly, people are eager to fund new business ideas, industries, and firms.

That's how it has worked in Shanghai, Dublin, Spain, Helsinki, Sydney, Montreal, Dubai, and Vancouver, all cities that have become hot in recent years. Vancouver is a particularly vivid example of the influence of outside money. It is the hottest real estate market in Canada, and it is one of the most vibrant cities in the world, yet nearly a third of its apartments and houses are empty. How can that be? Go back to the five years before 1999, when Hong Kong Chinese were looking for a place to put their money— and themselves—because they feared what would happen once Hong Kong passed from British control back to China's hands in 1999. Many acquired British passports, giving them the right to settle in any Commonwealth nation that would take them, including Canada and Australia. Many used that right to acquire homes as a hedge against the day when they would have to emigrate. When China's rule turned out to be more benign than expected, many Hong Kong Chinese kept their apartments as investments and sent their grown children to live and make money in Vancouver, giving them another base from which to exploit their capital.

This Hong Kong money helped to transform the city's skyline and to make it an attraction for talent. The perfection of processes to recover oil from Alberta's tar sands has also helped. Increasing amounts of that extracted oil are shipped to China, and the major port of shipment is Vancouver. Additionally, some oil experts believe that there there may be considerable amounts of oil in the rock formations surrounding Vancouver, making it a hotbed for exploration and investment. Finally, the harbor is the main entry point for goods from Asia coming into Canada. Its attractive climate and scenic landscape make it a terrific tourist destination, adding to the number of people who have decided to make Vancouver their home. Together, these dynamics have made Vancouver a venue for new capital, investment, and opportunity, all those empty apartments aside.

That doesn't mean that there are no worthwhile investments in the "colder" parts of the world. In Germany, which is just emerging from the economic doldrums of more than a decade, there are thousands of small to midsized companies available for purchase, because their owners are either retiring and the inheritors want to cash out, or they are stymied by Germany's strict labor laws in their efforts to restructure their companies (when a new owner takes over in Germany, he gets some latitude on renegotiating labor contracts that the old owners didn't have). This desire to sell is part of what has helped fuel both a boom in European equities in 2005 and an increase in mergers and acquisitions activity. Indeed, European M&A accounted for a quarter of the rise in European equity values in 2005, compared to only about 7 percent the year before. While European M&A is tapering off, the opportunities are excellent for a large M&A round to take place in the United States as well as in Japan. Japan may offer an even better opportunity than Germany. Most small Japanese companies are tied to larger ones via a process of association known as *keiretsu,* where the bank of a large industrial conglomerate holds the shares of the many smaller companies that act as suppliers to the conglomerate's own business units. Beginning in the 1990s, when Japan refused to reshape its bank capital according to the dictates of the Bank for International Settlements, its economy has stagnated, especially at the smaller-enterprise level. The BIS, which is located in Basel, Switzerland, is a global clearinghouse for the major international banks. It sets capital-adequacy standards for the banks of the nations that are members. In

1992, it raised what it called "tier 1 capital requirements"—the basic reserves that had to be held in cash—to 8 percent of a bank's assets. At that time Japan was in the midst of a huge real estate boom, and much of the major banks' capital had been lent out as mortgages and business loans, which were on the books as capital. Rather than call these loans, which might have precipitated a financial crash, Japanese banks chose to keep them on the books, effectively limiting their ability to lend for more than a decade. This illiquidity crippled Japan's economy. Japan is just emerging from its post-BIS economic meltdown. This decision left many of the smaller suppliers to Japan's giant *keiretsu* without access to adequate capital, and while many of these companies managed to soldier on, they are now at a stage when their owners are ready to sell off and retire. The number of private equity firms and M&A firms that are setting up shop in Japan is impressive, and the number of deals, beginning with real estate in 2003, is equally so. So it does not follow exactly that an area needs to be hot in order for it to be desirable for investors.

Often, cold is even better. The prices are cheaper, both for land and businesses, and often, government entities are desperately seeking to attract both capital and industry, and other entities are willing to give away the store in an effort to attract either one in order to keep a region's population from hitting the immigration trail. Generally, labor costs will be lower—if you can find a town or region with a well-trained population but without much in the way of local opportunity, you might have an investment gold mine. Smaller cities—such as Allentown and Harrisburg, Pennsylvania; Little Rock, Arkansas; Birmingham, Alabama; Albany, New York; and Dayton, Ohio, all once leading small industrial cities—now score highly in Richard Florida's rankings of potentially hot cities because of the efforts these towns have made to develop their educational and culture resources, what he calls a "knowledge base." All of them also have low-cost housing and ample facilities for industrial expansion.

Of course, you won't meet Michael Jackson or other celebrities in these small towns, the way you might if you live in Dubai, but then again, that's not why you're there. You want to increase the value of your investments, so when you are looking at companies, make it a practice to look at where they are expanding. If they have chosen areas that are hot or have concentrations of the talents they need, that's a promising sign. If they are expanding into areas where they can gain access to cheap, reliable labor, as the Japanese did in Tennessee and South Carolina, so much the better. You probably cannot take advantage of many of these place-specific opportunities directly, but you can and should follow the movements of companies as carefully as you follow investment flows. They are related.

The ability to generate flow mostly comes from outside, and today it is highly and increasingly dependent upon a form of beauty pageant. Now that cities know the rules by which Florida and others judge them, civic leaders go out of their way to create the appearance of investment-friendly circumstances. Sometimes the process is entirely self-generated and unexpected. When I was first working in Spain, the country was in transition from decades of rule under Franco to the re-establishment of monarchy, but as a modern democracy. To clarify the transition, the grandson of the last king was brought back and educated to take over. When Juan Carlos ascended to the throne in 1975, he surprised the world by liberalizing the nation and bringing about a reconciliation between the left and the right. He also opened Spanish society to investment by encouraging the new government to soften its restrictive banking and currency laws. Juan Carlos turned himself into his nation's top salesman, tirelessly visiting corporate leaders around the world, inviting them to set up shop in Spain. Many European and U.S. firms, attracted by Spain's cheap labor relative to other rates in Europe as well as the country's sunny climate and Mediterranean location (Spain was already a major tourist destination even in the Franco days and had already been receiving more tourists each year than Spain's total population), decided that a plant in Spain could improve productivity and their bottom lines. Moreover, as Spain's economy improved from all the new investment, it became a nation of 40 million increasingly prosperous consumers, much like the emerging Latin American and Asian economies today. Indeed, thirty years later, Spain's growth rate is still one of the highest in Europe, and its stock market performance has also been consistently strong. It has benefited immensely from its membership in the European Union, and although it now faces competition from Eastern European emerging nations, Spain is also a model for many of them. Moreover, its banks and companies now possess sufficient capital to put them on the acquisition trail, having recently made their mark as investors in telecommunications throughout Latin America and in infrastructure investments (Cintra Concesiones de Infraestructuras de Transporte of Madrid, Spain, in conjunction with Australia's Macquarie Bank) in the United States and Great Britain. As an example of how a nation can turn a laundry list of negatives into a success story worth emulating—and also a lesson for investors—Spain is hard to beat.

One of the most important lessons for investors from the Spanish experience is that at a certain point, pride in the past has to give way to the realities of the present and the possibilities of the future. Many companies have developed deeply embedded cultures and company "ways" of doing business that perhaps were successful once but now act as an impediment to innovation and growth, such as Hewlett-Packard (perhaps one reason it mired itself in an illegal investigation of its own board) or Ford. The same is true for you as an investor. You have habits that need to be changed if you are going to become more consistent.

Let's review. In evaluating an investment, location counts, but not as much as some people claim. Yes, it's fun to watch a commercial for the Kurdistan Development Corporation ("The Other Iraq"), which touts the relative calm and rapid development of the only part of the country where Sunnis and Shiites are not killing each other, but are you really going to invest there? If you are a genuine risk taker, perhaps. But in the main, you are going to invest where a confluence of events, people, capital, governance, and geopolitical stability lend themselves to the likelihood that if you put money in, you might get more money out. Remember that cold can be as good as hot if the right conditions for heating an environment might be made to exist, and by that I don't mean Richard Florida's recipe for cultural uplift, as appealing as it sounds. People like the four F's, and it's always nice to have a couple of good restaurants where you can go after a long day at the knowledge factory, but what people want just as much out of an environment is little or no crime, affordable housing, and good schools. Tracking where a company moves is as sound a way of marking progress as tracking monetary flows, and it's a lot easier, because companies are constantly touting their latest plant in a press release, while prying financial data out of a firm is something that even most Wall Street analysts have trouble doing.

CHAPTER 6

HERE *versus* THERE

Having just spent a couple of chapters getting ever more granular about making investment decisions from the perspective of a changing world, I'd like to pull back to a thirty-thousand-foot view, and look at the most fundamental binary: here versus there. It is not just a question of investment style, it's one of the fundamental questions of life. Is the grass really greener somewhere else, or do you pick a place where you are comfortable, make your stand, and exploit every possible advantage? Do you become a world-beater, or can you make yourself content as a local hero? A lot goes into the decision, either way.

"Follow the money" has been the rallying cry of reporters and prosecutors in recent years, but it should also be a rallying cry for investors. For now, the money I am talking about is foreign money invested in the United States. Foreign money is a reliable indicator of where the rest of the world is placing its bets. That doesn't mean that you should be investing in the same way, but it's always helpful to know which side of the trade you are on. The chart on page 44 tracks foreign investment in the U.S. market, both bonds (fixed income) and stocks (equities).

Clearly, the chart shows that foreigners were happy to buy our bonds; that's because we had entered a rising-interest-rate environment. Foreign governments, notably Asian nations, want U.S. Treasuries in order to maintain a fixed value for their currencies against the American dollar so that their export goods remain cheap and American consumers stay in a spending mood. On the other hand, the days when all the world's surplus capital found its way into U.S. equities—during the 1990s, more than 40 percent of U.S. stocks were held by foreigners—are long gone. The

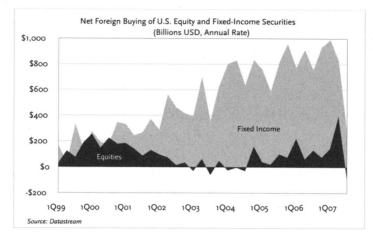

Net Foreign Buying of U.S. Equity and Fixed-Income Securities
(Billions USD, Annual Rate)

Source: Datastream

smart money has gone home to local stock markets. The rules may not be as favorable and the laws may not be as well enforced in small markets as they are here, but wealthy investors from abroad know their own markets better than they know ours, and, as they discovered to their chagrin after 2001, the markets here aren't as tightly regulated as they had been led to believe. The wave of corporate accounting scandals that brought down Enron, WorldCom, and a number of other giants, along with the U.S. subsidiaries of a number of European firms, such as Parmalat, and the subsequent reforms manifested by the Sarbanes-Oxley Act of 2002 have sent a signal to potential foreign investors in U.S. equities that they should seek their greener pastures elsewhere. Sarbanes-Oxley has also had a toxic effect on American investment. Many companies have used Sarbanes-Oxley as a rationale for going private, pulling out of the public equity market. Private equity firms, seeing the low prices of U.S. equities, have joined forces with many company managements to buy out companies, often paying little or no premium to the shareholders.

Unlike their ancestors, who often used the United States as a haven for money with no other place to go—local laws made investing difficult and payoffs problematic—today's foreign investors are younger and better educated, and they work in increasingly transparent environments. They are taking advantage of changes that have been long in coming, and their investment decisions led to a huge run-up in emerging market equities between 2003 and 2006. That and the carry trade.

The carry trade is a simple little trick for making lots of money. Find a country that has very low interest rates, such as Japan, where since 1992 rates were effectively zero, or the United States, where they were effectively zero between the end of 2001 and the middle of 2004, and borrow money long, say for a ten-year period. Now take that money, find a country with high interest rates (the situation in most emerging market nations following the financial meltdown of the late 1990s), and invest in its short-term bonds. As such economies reform and improve, their bond ratings shoot up and their interest rates begin to drop—slowly, at first, but then with increasing speed. When interest rates on bonds drop, their face value rises. It's the financial equivalent of the Dire Straits lyrics, "Get your money for nothin' and your chicks for free."

The theory worked so well that while professional bond traders were the early beneficiaries, by 2004 everyone who could put together the words *bond* and *fund* was selling carry-trade-based funds to ordinary investors. By early 2006, so much money had been invested in carry trades that both central bankers and professional bond traders like Bill Gross of PIMCO began to worry. For one thing, traders know that the carry trade carries the risk of exposure at both ends of the trade, since you have to eventually repay the money you borrowed and hedge against the possibility that the country in whose short-term paper you are investing will default or, worse, raise its rates. While default is bad enough, a rate rise can leave an investor in trouble at both ends of the trade, since you have to pay back cheap money with expensive money, which is another way of saying that you will lose money. Meanwhile, central bankers in many nations were growing nervous about the carry trade phenomenon, because the rise of cheap money was encouraging their legislators to become profligate. The fiscal stability that earns lower rates can easily encourage backsliding by encouraging nations to borrow more than they need, first under the guise of saving money on interest rates, then for development, and finally, when money gets really cheap, for endless helpings of political pork.

Meanwhile, investors were throwing their profits from carry trades back into the bond markets or into foreign equity markets. Stock and bond prices improved simultaneously, which, generally, they do not do. One of the main reasons that investors are urged to hold both stocks and bonds in their portfolios is precisely that they do not correlate well. Normally, when stocks go up, bonds go down, and vice versa. When stocks and bonds head up at the same time, it often means a contest between those investors who believe an economy is headed upward—the stock investors—and those who believe it is headed for a fall. Both cannot happen at the same time, so generally, one gives way to the other. And that's exactly what happened in 2006.

Emerging nations who were proud of their newly improved credit ratings decided that they wanted to hang on to those ratings, so they began raising their rates in conjunction with the central banks of large developed countries, beginning with the United States in 2004. (Raising rates, which dampens both legitimate economic activity and speculation, is a signal to bond investors that a government is going to pursue fiscal responsibility. One of the reasons given for U.S. prosperity between 1994 and 2000 was Treasury Secretary Robert Rubin's decision to press President Clinton for a balanced budget and Fed Chairman Alan Greenspan for higher interest rates. Both complied, the economy and stock markets shot skyward, and the budget came into balance after years of deficits.) The smartest investors unwound their carry trades—they sold their short positions, repaid their loans, and sold off their equities—and caused a stampede for the door on the part of less-sophisticated investors who suddenly realized that their emerging market equity and bond funds had begun to tumble. Nothing had changed in reality—countries with good credit and strong economies remained so, and their markets are beginning to recover—but after the tech debacle of 2000, investors who were just starting to rebuild their portfolios discovered the perils of here versus there.

Except for one thing. While Americans were pulling their cash out of *there*, they were not putting it into markets *here*. Investors in the United States, battered by the bursting of the Internet and telecom bubbles, have lost much of their confidence in the equity markets; as energy prices rise, a futile war in Iraq drags on, and yet another corporate scandal emerges—the latest involving the backdating of stock options to enrich corporate executives at the expense of shareholders (it's always at the expense of shareholders)—many Americans, especially those nearing retirement, are convinced that there are better things to do with their money than invest in U.S. equities, despite rising earnings per share since early 2002. There is no mechanism in the U.S. corporate world for executives to express contrition, as corporate heads do in Japan (there, they bow deeply, apologize to those they have befouled, and move on, with a little compensation thrown in). Here, we have only the legal system. Over the long haul, this constant scarpering from the law by the very people held up as role models has made investors understandably cynical.

Convinced that the grass is not so green over here and having been ensnared by a little crabgrass and poison ivy over there, what's an investor to do? The answer has been around for generations, but many American investors still don't understand it. It's called protection, and it is simple. Most people, if they purchase stocks, buy them naked, without either a put or call attached. People who believe they are being sophisticated might place a stop-loss order; that is, if the stock falls more than, say, 20 percent within a particular time frame, the brokerage house automatically sells it, thereby limiting the loss. But here's the problem: First, most investors set their stop-loss orders too high. Let's say a stock is selling for two standard deviations above its historical price, and higher than the sector in which it trades. At two standard deviations, it means that more than 78 percent of all owners of the stock are on one side of the trade, with only 22 percent on the other (78 percent are likely to sell, only 22 percent are willing to commit to the possibility of a further rise). This means that there is more than three times as much downside risk as upside potential left in the stock, or, in other words, three times the chance that it will fall before it rises further. If it rises to three standard deviations, then you are at 96 percent on the wrong side; at four, you are at 99 percent (this is where many emerging market equities were when the market began to fall in the spring of 2006, and where it was in the United States when the Internet and telecom bubbles burst). If you wait for a 20 percent fall before you sell in a two-standard-deviation world, you are almost all the way back to neutral, which means you probably didn't make any money on the trade, and when you add in buy and sell commissions and the time value of holding on to the stock—the money you might have made investing it in something safer, such as cash—you have probably either lost money or done no better than break even. That is never going to get you the kind of returns you deserve.

On the other hand, you can buy a put or call on the stock when you purchase it, or both. A call is an option that gives you the right to purchase a given stock at a specific price within a designated period of time. A put, on the other hand, gives you the right to sell a given stock at a specific price within a designated period of time. Puts and calls are designed to add flexibility to markets, so why not take advantage of them? In purchasing a put or a call, you pay a fee for the privilege of getting the contract, but you gain what I call insurance. You use calls if you want to profit from a rise in stock prices but also avoid sharp losses if the stock suddenly heads south. Holding the call gives you two options: If the market advances, you can buy the stock at the lower price quoted in the call and then sell it at a profit. If the market declines, you can exercise your option not to buy the stock, thereby avoiding a major loss. In that case, the only expense is the cost of the option.

However, if you discover a stock you want to purchase because it looks as if it has some upside potential, but it could fall catastrophically, you can purchase a put to gain the profit from a fall in the stock price. Put another way, if you hold a put for a stock that declines in price, you can sell the stock at the higher price quoted in the put, thereby profiting by the amount the stock declines from the put price. If the stock price rises, the only money you lose, again, is the cost of the option. Puts and calls are generally written for one, two, three, or six months, although any period over twenty-one days is accepted by the New York Stock Exchange. A straddle and a spread are combinations of puts and calls occasionally used by sophisticated investors. In a more general sense, the term *call* may refer to any demand for payment.

So why don't investors do this more often? I believe that it is for the same reason that they increasingly purchase mutual funds instead of choosing their own stocks and bonds. Investing to gain a better-than-average return requires real work over an extended period of time. Americans are no longer just buy-and-hold investors; they tend to be buy-and-forget investors. Managing puts and calls is difficult work, because you have to pay close attention to the markets. Most people have other things to do than monitor their money. (Since the late 1980s, American companies have transferred an increasing portion of their costs directly to consumers. You now pay for the privilege of booking an airline ticket, whereas the airlines used to pay travel agents. You spend your time arguing with your health insurance provider about claims that used to be paid routinely. I could go on, but the point is that Americans may be the most time-pressured people on the planet, so I have sympathy for those who say they don't have enough time to manage their investments. But this is one of those areas where you really *do* have to make time.) In addition, Americans who have begun investing since the end of World War II— almost all of us have had mostly up years. Americans do not have the experience of Asians, Latin Americans, or Europeans, who have repeatedly seen their investments wiped out by inflation, war, speculation, and scandal. Such events happen in the United States, but much less often.

The other factor that inhibits Americans from buying insurance on their stocks is that they learned the wrong lesson in 1987, when the stock markets suddenly collapsed in October of that year. A particular set of circumstances involving the exercise of options occurred—since called "the triple witching hour"—when a group of short-, medium-, and long-term option trades expired simultaneously, spooked the market (overvalued to begin with), and sent the Dow and the S&P 500 off a cliff. But there was nothing wrong with the underlying economy. In fact, it was improving rapidly. So those investors who had the courage to hold on to their stocks prospered, as did those who purchased more stocks at massively depressed prices. I remember that period, how the business magazines were talking about a "new depression"—and how little sense it made. Investors quickly figured that out, and buy and hold became the rallying cry of American investment. Had you had the courage never to sell, you would have been rewarded with a 13 percent average annual gain. That lesson turned American investors into stubborn goats. When the markets tanked in 2000 and 2001, many large institutional investors sold, but most individuals refused to be swayed by events. The new accepted wisdom was that the markets would return. Now, in early 2008, the Dow Industrials have finally retraced their losses, but the NASDAQ is still down nearly 50 percent, and the S&P 500 is only near its last high.

Foreign investors, who are less patient, quietly decamped for the greener pastures of home. A few smart Americans went with them. The lessons for foreign markets, not surprisingly, are pretty much the same as for your home market. Is the government stable? Is the currency rising in value? Are companies making their profits from growth or financial manipulation? Is the population's income rising while the nation's current account deficit is falling? This is a sure sign that people are saving more than they are spending, which means that capital spending will rise. If so, you probably have a good bet for making an investment that will not blow up in your face. Look at Brazil. It has managed to pay off its loans to the International Monetary Fund years ahead of schedule. It has a rising trade surplus and both falling government deficits and interest rates. The government is both popular and reasonably honest. Nearly every sector of Brazil's growing economy is hitting on all cylinders. When emerging markets ran into trouble in June 2006, Brazil's stocks and bonds headed downward along with everyone else's—but then they bounced back. Why? Because knowledgeable investors had separated Brazil from the rest of the pack and put their money back into the country, leaving the stocks of riskier nations, such as Middle Eastern stocks, at the altar.

If you can train yourself to become an alert investor, you have a chance to become a successful one. If you are willing to pay attention to the wealth you are managing, you can avoid the pain that comes from not doing so. It is so difficult to recover if you have fallen behind that you might as well throw in the towel and start purchasing lottery tickets. That's about the chance you're going to have of making significant money from your investments if you are asleep.

I tell people that the most important step they have to take in getting a new idea off the ground is to find north, and then head that way. What I mean is that if you spend too much time trying to figure out where you are, you will never figure out where you have to go. Pick a direction and head there. You will soon learn whether or not you are going the wrong way, if you remain alert, and then you will be able to make course corrections quickly and when the error rate doesn't cost you so much.

Let's review. In choosing here versus there, you are looking for a combination of risk and reward that you can live with. It is always tempting to see the rewards that come with investing in a different security or a different country, but you also have to teach yourself how to be alert to the risks. At the same time, you do not want to be a buy-and-hold or buy-and-forget investor. Here versus there means learning how to strike a proper balance between what you are currently doing and what you have to do in order to become a more consistent investor. Your choice.

PART II

A CHANGING INVESTOR

In the last chapter of the first section, I stated my belief that people need to take responsibility for their money. If you buy the idea that the world has changed and that the investment strategies and tactics that stood you well over the past three or four decades no longer work, then why would you stick with them? Clearly, you have to retool yourself to put your thinking in line with new market realities. But how?

People reshape themselves all the time. They enter into relationships and end them. They start families and change jobs and, increasingly, careers. Change is a central component of living. Indeed, even if you refuse to accept that, you are aging from the moment you are born, whether you do anything about it or not. How you choose to live is the question. Investing is only a means to an end, a way to give you more options and choices during your life and, if you are successful enough to be able to leave behind an estate, to provide more options for your children and grandchildren beyond you.

In our post-9/11 world, we must learn how to manage risk. We always had to manage risk, but it was not until after 9/11 that most Americans began to take the idea more seriously. When my nephew Nick was a teenager, we took a drive together to see my grandmother—his great-grandmother. She lived miles from the nearest village. In fact—this was twenty years ago—as we drove the last fifty miles to her house, there wasn't a single gas station. We had been on the road for a while and were running low on fuel, so I told Nick that we were going to stop and gas up. He asked me why. It would be fun, he said, to see if we could make it all the way to Grandma's on whatever was left in the tank.

I thought about that and said, "Okay. Let's consider this a risk management problem. If we don't gas up and make it to Grandma's, we haven't lost anything. But if we don't make it, we're going to have to hike for several miles until we find a friendly stranger, or else wait for hours until we can get a tow, and then we're still going to have to buy gas. So the downside risk of not filling up is tremendous. Whether we fill up now or later, the upside is still the same, because we still have to pay for the gas either way. Buying gas now, before we attempt to complete the journey, is free insurance, because we were going to spend the money anyway." My nephew was a little disappointed in me for not sharing his sense of adventure, but he learned something about managing risk that day.

Many investors are so busy keeping an eye on the number—how much they are earning or losing—that they forget to focus on *why* it is happening. But it is the *why* that determines what is going to happen next. If you have trouble with this concept, think about a game like Texas hold'em. How you bet is as important as the cards you have in your hand, sometimes more so. If you don't pay attention to the betting patterns, you can lose even though you have what would otherwise be a winning hand.

Risk management influences nearly everything you do in life. Millions of people choose not to maintain health insurance, for example, hoping that the premiums they avoid paying will not turn around and bite them in the case of an unexpected medical disaster. The majority of the people who forgo medical insurance are young and single, as opposed to the millions more with families who simply decide that they cannot afford health insurance and so are forced into risky behavior. Forgoing insurance in most cases is an example of poor risk management, because there are too many elements beyond your control.

An example of sound risk management is the current incarnation of Tiger Woods. When he first began playing professional golf a decade ago, Woods depended upon his strength, his shot-making ability, and a willingness to take big risks when needed. As his wins piled up, though, he realized that the practices that had carried him through to his early victories would become bad habits over time, so he changed his swing coach and began to reconstruct his game. Now, when Tiger Woods plays, he not only plays to win, but he also concentrates on not losing, working hard to hit fairways and greens in regulation so that he does not give shots to par back to the field. By staying at or near par and by getting the ball reasonably close to the pin, Woods has a sufficient number of birdie opportunities so that even if he only makes a couple per game, he moves into contention. This is risk management at its finest, and it has put Tiger Woods in a position to surpass Jack Nicklaus's record of eighteen major tournament wins.

Sound risk management is also what investors need to look for in investments. It is no longer sufficient for a company to be profitable. In a world of increasing competition, where new challenges emerge all the time, how a company behaves on a day-to-day basis is as important as the huge mergers and acquisitions it makes. As too many companies have proved, it is the small things, the little failures to execute, the cutting of corners, that undermine trust in a company and ultimately diminish the bottom line, not to mention its share price. Small daily decisions, improperly made, are like the tiny, nearly weightless, nearly invisible snowflakes that eventually gather into an avalanche. You look at the devastation afterward, and you have to marvel. How could something as evanescent and lighthearted as a snowflake wreak so much havoc? Poor risk management is the answer, for both business and the avalanche. The business fails to manage the small issues until they snowball out of control; the same is true of the ski basin operator who fails to pay attention to the character of snow.

You, the investor, have to manage risks today in a way that you never did before. As we noted earlier, there was a time when the economy was expanding at a fairly constant rate, when there were millions of new entrants into the stock market to provide a sustained lift in prices. Now the U.S. market in particular is fairly mature. Global investors have other choices, other venues, for their money. They choose growth over the status quo, and even though the risks abroad may appear somewhat greater, with each passing day that an emerging nation keeps its deficits in line and the United States does not, with each day that an emerging nation raises the GDP of its citizens and the United

States does not, with each day that an emerging nation provides more investment opportunities and stimulates new business development in ways that the United States no longer does, the risk gap between that emerging nation and the United States narrows. At a certain point, the here-versus-there question gets answered without it ever being consciously asked. Even the laziest investor will eventually figure out what many others already have: that many U.S. stocks are not providing the opportunities for growth that they once did.

Will this always be the case? In the late 1980s and early 1990s, many analysts in the business press were making the same argument, that the ability of the United States to grow and prosper was over. They were wrong then, so one has to ask whether they could be wrong again. It would be silly of me or anyone to say that the United States is finished. Ours is the largest, most resilient economy in the world. Despite stagnation in overall new business start-ups—the number has remained fairly constant at around four million a year, even with a rising population— we still start more new businesses than the rest of the world put together. We still possess more middle-class consumers than anyone, and for that reason Asian and Latin American nations are still willing to prop up the dollar with the scant wages of their own citizens, all for the right to sell their products to us. But at a certain point, prosperous home markets in Asia will become faster-growing venues for sales than the mature and increasingly tenuous markets of the United States. While we are purchasing more and more cheaply made Chinese goods at Wal-Mart, the increasingly wealthy Chinese are buying upscale consumer goods in shopping centers in Shanghai, Hong Kong, and Guangzhou.

Another sign that our own stock markets are in a mature phase is the sudden move by the New York Stock Exchange to take itself public, to create its own products, to go on the M&A trail, and to purchase foreign exchanges. After an explosion in volume during the late 1980s and early 1990s driven largely by data-processing technology—the sheer ability to handle more trades at the same time that Americans were becoming big purchasers of stocks through mutual funds and their 401(k) plans—volume, which is what earns the NYSE its income, has leveled off since 2000. In order to drive volume, the NYSE needs new products and new ways to entice customers to purchase, just like any of the companies that list on it. As a result, the NYSE has been forced to look abroad for new products, just as new investors have done.

In this risk-defined world, investors and ordinary people alike have become more wary. You should not lock yourself up in your room and draw the curtains, or build a panic room in your next house. The United States is not yet a banana republic, if only because a sufficient number of people still believe the United States is a nation of opportunity. There have always been more new business start-ups in a declining economy than in a rising economy. Why? Because people who have lost their jobs are thrown back on their own resources and have to screw up their courage and take a chance. The fledgling business might fail—in fact, most fail within five years—but the prospect of earning a living on your own when jobs are scarce is always better than the prospect of no job at all. In a rising job market, the opportunistic urge wanes, as people look for the security of a steady job and a regular paycheck, and the benefits that used to attend both.

There is a similar pattern with investing. In good economic times, investors concentrate on fundamentals, examining both absolute and relative earnings, and ratios such as price/earnings and price/sales, or even price/book value, as determinants of the relative value of one stock over another. But when times are uncertain, irrational exuberance takes over, and routine stock analysis flies out the window. Investors begin to read tea leaves. What is the Fed going to do next month? How will the markets respond? Will consumer confidence rise or fall? Is the price of oil headed up or down? What about gold? Should I buy it or hoard it?

Questions such as these tend to come to the fore when uncertainty prevails. Ordinary uncertainty is that combination of political and geopolitical events that knocks markets sideways and sends investors into a panic. Often, that panic results from real events. Hurricane Katrina damages the oil platforms of the Gulf of Mexico, cutting off a nearby supply and forcing consumers to scramble for more-distantly-imported oil. Or perhaps it is the downturn in oil supplies from Iraq due to the ongoing conflict there. Whatever the cause, these uncertainties are the result of events in the real world.

Increasingly, it seems, uncertainty is expanding due to notional events. What is a notional event? It is something that might or might not happen but has sufficient probability that you have to accept it as if it were real. Before 9/11, the idea that terrorists would hijack four planes and ram them into buildings was a low-probability event, an idea so far off the scale of antiterrorist planners that when the event actually took place, the first reaction of the military air traffic controllers who are supposed to police and defend the skies above the United States was that it must be some sort of exercise or drill. By the time they realized that it wasn't a drill and scrambled fighter jets in response, all four planes that had been hijacked had already crashed, three of them having hit their intended targets. Now hijackings are highly notional events indeed—even the rumor of one is enough to send authorities at airports around the world into a high-security alert.

In the risk-driven world in which we must now live and react, notional events have as much priority in our consciousnesses and decision making as real events, and sometimes more. Following the outbreak of SARS in Asia and Canada in 2002, the possibility of a pandemic that might kill millions was raised from remote to notional, so that when the World Health Organization talks about an avian flu pandemic, as it has for the past three years, companies and institutions are forced to spend a small fortune planning for the eventuality, even if it never comes.

When did notional behavior come to dominate our thinking and our tolerance for risk? I can't be sure, but I think it began with Y2K, an event that now has been all but forgotten. A simple thing, really, Y2K was a computer accident waiting to happen. Computer chips from the early 1980s and 1990s had built-in clocks that went only to the end of 1999, at which time they would shift back to 1900. Since this would not square with the real date, it was imagined computers would go into a tizzy and shut down. Elevators would fall in their shafts, planes would fall out of the sky, stock market transactions would be wiped out, and patients sick in their hospital beds would not receive their medications and die, all, so the theory went, because so many critical functions had become computer-dependent. Companies around the world spent more than $500 billion to retool their computers, with most of that money spent in the United States, where the fear was greatest. When nothing happened at the stroke of midnight on December 31, 1999, a lot of people laughed nervously and shrugged their shoulders, happy to have dodged a notional bullet.

But remember: more than $500 billion had been spent to construct a shield against a bullet that was never fired. In the investment world, we live by what is called "the law of unintended consequences," and one of the unintended consequences of Y2K was a dearth of computer spending in the early years of the twenty-first century. Much of that was explained away by the bursting of the technology bubble in 2000, but which came first, the spending deficit or the bursting of the bubble? It was the diversion of funds from advanced technology into safeguarding old technology that may have proved to be the backbreaking straw. The information technology industry is only just beginning to recover, making it a nonstarter for investors for the past six years.

The rise of any number of notional events that need to be treated as real has added to our level of uncertainty and risk, but that's hardly the last of it. There is yet another category of uncertainty, the *visible yet incomprehensible,* that drives investors up the wall and leads them to avoid putting their money to work. Visible yet incomprehensible events surround you. What to do about pension and Social Security reforms is a visible yet incomprehensible event. Everyone knows the problem, but nobody wants to suggest a solution, because any solution is political, and nobody wants to be on the losing end where pensions are concerned. So nothing gets done as the problem gets worse and worse. The same goes for a solution in the Middle East. There is no solution that will satisfy all parties, and as long as that is so, there can be no lasting peace, let alone a permanent one. There are many more such visible yet incomprehensible problems, and they are a sore vexation for investors, because every time they pop up, they appear as notional problems or even real ones, and both of these categories require real time, real money, and real effort to control, not to mention raising risk levels as investors prepare for an eventuality they know may never arrive. Visible yet incomprehensible problems sap the most energy, divert the most attention, and are most likely to send investors in the wrong direction.

Take pension reform. If it ever came to pass, and pensions were made portable—*you* would own your pension plan, not your company, and take it with you as you changed jobs—as they are in Great Britain, it might mean a huge boon for the insurance and financial services industry. So when Congress began to take up the issue in 2005, the stocks of those sectors immediately rose, only to fall back again as pension reform was shelved for yet another year. As of this writing, a bill has passed Congress that changes the funding of pensions, but it provides no real relief for companies that have defined contribution plans, as do most old-line industrial firms, such as General Motors. Their traditional path to pension reform, declaring bankruptcy and throwing their pension liability onto the Federal Pension Benefit Guarantee Corporation, has now been cut off, and these companies must fund their pensions by the end of 2009. So does that make them an opportunity, as the date for final conformity has been set, or a liability, as it raises the risk that many firms might go bankrupt due to pension pressure? That's a level of risk assessment that even professionals will have difficulty with, and many of their answers will be wrong.

American investors are uncomfortable with that kind of risk management. After all, an entire generation of investors has been schooled in the idea that they are *not* smart enough to manage their own money and must depend upon the experts who run mutual funds. That most funds underperformed standard benchmarks when other economic and market conditions were much better than they are today should have given investors pause. That didn't happen. Today, with risk levels much higher and the need to sort through investment possibilities much more critical and time-consuming, neither investors nor fund managers are particularly adept at distinguishing the good, the bad, and the ugly.

How, then, do you become a better risk manager? The answer lies in figuring out what the risks are and then knowing how to asses the risks once you have identified them. Let's take the first part of the problem. Put aside the notional and the visible yet incomprehensible risks for a moment. They are all going to affect the market, but if you can concentrate instead on what is real and will happen, you will have knocked down a significant portion of the possible risks. Those risks haven't gone away, but by putting them to one side, you can assess a smaller set more intelligently and then come back to the others within a better-defined context.

I assess risks by examining the forces that I know will affect the future and placing them together in "buckets" that encompass several common ideas. Right now, I work with only four real buckets, plus one that has all of the visible yet incomprehensible threats—the notional as well as the hypothetical—lumped together. The four buckets are labeled "Demographics," "Economy, Financial Markets, and Imbalances," "Energy," and "Path of Reform/Big Emerging Markets." If you either take them separately or put them together in combination, you can come up with a huge variety of investment rationales that will allow you to assess stocks, bonds, and business opportunities.

Demographics

One of the nice things about this bucket is that it starts with a lot of well-verified information. Demographers have information on birth and death rates, life expectancies, causes of death and disease, eating habits, education, employment, and hundreds of other subjects. Demographic knowledge forms the basis for almost all decision making regarding the economy. After all, an economy is nothing more than the actions of large numbers of people consuming and working. The decisions of what and how much food, clothing, shelter, entertainment, medical care, education, and all sorts of other things to buy is the fundamental determinant of success for companies.

Economy, Financial Markets, and Imbalances

The next bucket tracks the flow of money and demand around the system. It's one thing to need food and shelter, but such things have to be paid for, and money is the medium of exchange between your labor and that of someone else. Money is a neutral medium, as all money is the same, fungible, no matter who earns it or how it is earned. This bucket also tracks the way people feel about their investments. People feel differently about money when they are making it than when they are losing it. This field of study is called behavioral finance, and it is becoming increasingly important in figuring out how to make investments. Tracking money flows also puts you into the world of currencies. Ideally, investments where the stock or bond is denominated in a currency that is rising relative to others provide investors with an extra kick. For example, in 2005, if you were fearful about the U.S. economy, you could have bought, let's say, a $10,000 U.S. Treasury bill and received an absolutely safe 4 percent return. But for no additional risk, you could have purchased Canadian Treasury notes that were paying 6 percent. Rising energy prices and a demand for Canada's vast natural resources pushed the Canadian dollar to par with the U.S. dollar by the end of 2007. So while your $10,000 T-bill paid you $800 in interest (4 percent a year), your 6 percent Canadian Treasury note gave you a huge currency kicker—so much so that you would have made more than 25 percent a year with no more risk than buying a T-bill. Currencies matter, and you should factor them into your investment decisions.

ENERGY

Energy is the story of our time. While oil prices have dropped from their recent highs, any number of factors could send prices shooting upward again. How to secure steady supplies of energy—at any price— becomes a crucial driver for any economy. Once you have it, keeping it—oil nationalism is rising, and Venezuela, Iran, and others are be- coming increasingly disputatious about who their customers are— becomes another problem, and then making it clean—solving all of the environmental concerns surrounding carbon-based energy—becomes still another concern for investors. And of course, there is the question of what to do with all the money. Oil-producing nations will wind up with a surplus of about $450 billion in 2006. That surplus will be recycled in some fashion, either as investments in infrastructure for the short haul or as investments for savings, probably in the form of foreign currency–denominated stocks and bonds, for the long haul. No great influx of oil money has yet bolstered U.S. equities, as in the late 1970s, the last time there was a huge surplus of oil capital in need of recycling. What's different this time? Before, we welcomed Middle Eastern money with open arms. Now, with Islamist fundamentalism responsible for a rise in terror attacks, U.S. and European authorities are skeptical of Middle Eastern investments. Investors from that region have quickly figured this out and, loath to go where they are not welcome, have chosen to put their money in—you guessed it—emerging markets, especially China and India.

Conventional energy investing isn't the only path you can choose. When oil was cheap, alternatives were relatively expensive, on a cost-per-oil-equivalent basis. But now, with oil dear, alternatives look increasingly inexpensive—ethanol, wind, hydroelectric, coal, and above all, nuclear. None of the problems associated with any of these alternatives has gone away, but when you look at the attendant problems to be solved, what is the difference between, say, carbon sequestration for millennia and radioactive waste sequestration for the same period? The carbon has to be taken out of the air to reduce global warming, while the nuclear waste has to be stored until it cools down. Both are disposal problems. Now nuclear looks like an increasingly better bet, especially if coal usage ramps up.

Energy in any form is only useful and valuable if it can be converted into some form of work, so investments in energy infrastructure must also increase. Whether it's oil or gas pipelines or double-hulled supertankers, railcars for coal and the rails they travel over, additions to the world's electricity grid or new hydroelectric dams, the world needs an energy infrastructure to meet its increased demand for energy. Since the lack of infrastructure is the choke point of development—think blackouts and electricity shortages in China or, for that matter, blackouts here in the United States, as in the summer of 2006—these investments have a strong degree of durability and will pay off for years to come.

Path of Reform/Big Emerging Markets

The path of reform/big emerging markets is a theme that begins with the fall of the Soviet Union in 1991 and the tearing down of the Berlin Wall two years earlier. It is a theme about not politics but rather the alternative to politics. Back when there was a well-defined political West and East, the "nonaligned" nations—most of the countries in Asia, Africa, and Latin America—discovered that it was easier to extract money from the USSR and the United States by threatening alliance with one side or the other than to implement economic and governmental reforms that would boost domestic incomes. The corruption that comes with large cash payments and grandiose development projects was suddenly blown aside by a critical need to reform, as the funding began to dry up at the end of the Cold War. Nations that had splurged away a generation of wealth sobered up, hired transformation experts like Harvard's Jeffrey Sachs (now at Columbia University) or, if they were uncomfortable with taking advice from the West, a more congenial expert like Peru's Hernando de Soto. These countries then began the painful process of instituting the rule of law, property protection, and sound banking and financial procedures. Doing so made their nations attractive to the capital that was once provided without strings by western leaders desperate to win the Cold War.

At about the same time that this path of reform was developing, researchers at the U.S. Department of Commerce began to examine these newly emerging, formerly nonaligned nations and noticed that the largest ones all had a number of features in common, the most important of which, from an American perspective, was that as per capita GDP rose toward a middle-class standard, these nations became huge importers of western goods. The French and Italians might fill the trendy shops of Bangkok, Shanghai, and São Paulo with fashion and shoes, but the Americans began to sell Poland, Egypt, Indonesia, Brazil, South Africa, South Korea, Thailand, India, and China billions of dollars' worth of electronics, medical equipment, jet airplanes, and computer hardware, in addition to agricultural commodities. This trend continues even today, although nations such as China and India are increasingly turning the tables and selling more to us than we sell to them. But, of course, that creates its own opportunities, in the form of the emerging market equities that investors have put their money into over the past three or four years.

The path of reform/big emerging markets bucket has all sorts of pieces in it that create investment opportunities, such as infrastructure plays—all those goods require ports, airports, railroads, and roads to move along, as well as the usual infrastructures needed to support an increasingly urbanized population—but there are also interesting investments in rising consumer demand, agriculture, and even global political realignment. Nature may abhor a vacuum, but the political world abhors hegemony, and the longer the United States has remained the lone superpower, the more other nations have noticed how much the idea of hegemony bothers them. Further, as other nations develop, they have a tendency to move in their own directions. While showing U.S. films in their cinemas may have played well in the 1990s, big emerging nations—and lots of smaller ones as well—now see it as culturally imperative to have a film industry. They are just as likely to follow the direction of Bollywood as Hollywood, or even their own way entirely, knowing that their films will find a home on the U.S. independent film circuit and bring yet more dollars back. And what is true of film is also true of music, fashion, and design, all generators of high-value hard currency.

Now, what makes the idea of thematic buckets especially valuable to you as a tool for reducing risk is that not only is most of the information that goes into the buckets widely available, but the ideas in the buckets can also be easily combined to generate yet more investment possibilities. Take the example of high oil prices. You could have made money in oil by investing in any of the major oil companies, and you would have done quite nicely. But if you had combined an energy play with the path of reform, you would have seen that the economies of some nations, those well along the path to reform, got a better boost from their oil wealth than those further behind. The stock markets of those countries did better, their bond spreads dropped more rapidly, their real estate markets performed better, and their citizens had more money to consume on just the kinds of products that American companies most want to sell. Add a demographic idea like education to the mix, and you can imagine all kinds of new possibilities for profitable investments.

You can also combine thematic buckets to avoid risk. Let's take the same two, energy and emerging markets. If you spent some time learning about emerging markets, you might have noticed that in some of them, the rule of law was less developed than in others. This might have made you more cautious in investing in these markets, even though those nations might also have had oil. It would make you even more leery about alternative investments in those nations, such as real estate or agricultural commodities.

What about a nation that has a strong path of reform and rule of law but no energy resources? A good example of such a nation is Singapore, which instead of energy exploits its talented, well-educated labor pool. With its position as a port servicing both the Pacific and Indian Oceans, Singapore has become a major trade center. Its docks can unload cargo ships in record time, and its airport has the fastest turnaround time for planes in the world. Singapore has now begun to exploit its efficiency by becoming a refiner, emulating Rotterdam, another port city, in extracting value from the energy that passes through the port. Now it is even shaking off its straightlaced ways to become a center for gambling and entertainment, as it tries to lure some of the billions of dollars passing through the hands of the Chinese who currently flock to Singapore to shop.

Using these thematic buckets, you can gain a better understanding of the world, and through that understanding begin to get a better handle on risks and what goes into decision making. In the chapters that follow, we are going to take a look at the binaries that directly influence you, the investor, as you face a changing world and changing markets.

CHAPTER 7

FEAR *versus* GREED

What drives investment decision making? It's actually not complicated. Most of the time, markets are governed either by fear or greed. Below is a chart I show to clients: capital allocation decisions are directed toward preservation strategies, growth strategies, or neither (which manifests as hesitation or opportunity). Our feelings, indicated by the arrows, swing back and forth between fear and greed. As the needle swings from fear to greed and vice versa, people don't know whether to switch from a strategy of preservation to a strategy of growth. They settle for hesitation. Not certain whether fear or greed is governing their markets, they wait too long and thus miss the opportunity.

In the years since the collapse of the Internet and telecom bubbles in 2000 and the post-9/11 rise of terrorism as a global factor, fear has been the prime mover in the major global equity markets. Many investors would rather keep their money in cash than put it to work in stocks, so that while markets have come back from their post-2001 lows, they are

CAPITAL ALLOCATION DECISIONS

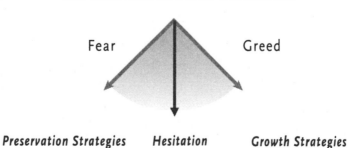

Fear   Greed

Preservation Strategies   **Hesitation**   **Growth Strategies**

only just beginning to move past their pre-2000 highs, despite record earnings from many companies and good performances from many more. Many investors know that the fear factors that drove them into preservation strategies no longer exist, but they continue to hear enough bad news that they hesitate to commit more than a minimal amount of their capital to growth.

Someone once said that being successful in markets is not really about what you know; it's about guessing right often enough about what other people think they know. You might be pretty certain that the terrorist threat to the United States and the rest of the developed world is ebbing rather than increasing, despite news that pops up from time to time about terrorist cells here or there. You might choose, on that basis, to get out of companies that make security equipment and into a sector with strong growth prospects, such as technology. But what you believe is not what everyone else believes. Most people, including many experts, would tell you that the terror threat—not the reality, mind you, but the notional threat—might be increasing, so that while you are bailing out of security equipment, the sector records a 99 percent boost over the past five years against only a partial recovery for the S&P 500. You might be "right," but you are fighting *sentiment*.

Fear and greed are both sentiments and as such are based upon the collective beliefs of all investors. There are a number of good books about behavioral finance that you can read, and, in periods when the markets cannot find direction, an understanding of the ways sentiment influences investors and the factors that influence the development of sentiment is useful. Among the factors that most influence fear is the prospect of change. At the moment, we live in a very fluid world. There are the normal demographic changes of aging taking place: the front edge of the dominant baby boom cohort born between 1945 and 1965 is beginning to reach its retirement years. That generation is losing its role as the dominant force in American decision making, and it is afraid that the future is going to lack the growth of privilege to which the boomers have grown accustomed. Within the boomers there is one subgroup that is even more afraid of change: the religious right. Without making any value judgments about whether their fears are reasonable or not, it is safe to say that this group perceives a constant assault on its values and believes that only a retreat to more traditional roles will save the country from chaos.

Then there is the population at large, which does fear a lot of the notional threats—menaces like terrorism, the possibility that Iran or North Korea will eventually develop nuclear weapons, avian flu, AIDS, a destructive computer virus, or perhaps the loss of their jobs should their company decide to outsource. Or it could be any one of a thousand other things, ranging from the health and welfare of one's own family all the way up to the most cosmic. It's not that the world is filled with millions of Chicken Littles. It is that for almost everyone, some part of the sky really is falling.

Fear is a natural phenomenon. It helps you sharpen your survival instincts. When humans were still creatures of the wilderness, it took sharp wits, sensory acuity, and speed to stay ahead of natural predators. In this endeavor, humanity probably was not as good as its cousins, the great apes, which is why we were forced to move out onto the plains of the savannah. There, our vision sharpened, and we learned to see our enemies from miles away. We learned how to protect ourselves. Whenever we failed, natural selection kicked in, and over time, fear became a survival tool. We use it still. Almost always our first reaction to that which we don't understand, fear forces us to pull back until we can regain enough courage to move forward. But if we have to confront too many fears at the same time, we become paralyzed, either by the fears themselves or by the decisions we might have to make. Paralysis by analysis.

How do you overcome your fears? I'm not a psychologist, so I can't really answer that question easily. But in investment decision making, you should take what I describe as the civilized approach. Modern civilizations rest on two foundations: engineering and insurance. Engineering is about applying science to real-world problems, but more to the point, it is about taking large, complicated problems and breaking them down into smaller, more easily digestible problems, solving those, and then constructing a large solution that includes many smaller solutions. Insurance is simply the ability to lay off risk, by aggregating small probabilities—the odds that you will be hit by a car are very small, but the odds that someone at some point will be hit by a car and require medical attention are large. If we aggregate lots of small risks, the cost of paying off any one of them is also small.

So first, take your large problem, and break it down. Let's say, for example, that you have $100,000 to invest. The conventional wisdom says that you should allocate some of it to stocks, some to bonds, some to cash, and perhaps even a bit to an alternative investment, such as real estate. Asset allocation is a reasonable approach—an engineering approach, you might say—because it breaks down the large problem into a set of smaller ones. But have you really laid off any risk? Yes, because when stocks go up, bonds generally go down, and vice versa. Sometimes both are up or down and real estate is busy doing its own thing. Real estate correlates somewhat to interest rates at large but more closely to location and local economies, so while the general economy might be down, local real estate values might be rising. And, of course, in times of fear, it is always good to have some cash. But what have you really done in your asset allocation process?

Well, first, you have to choose which stocks to buy. Are there good defensive stocks? Often in falling markets, "necessity" sectors such as pharmaceuticals and food do well, because people worry more about their individual health and well-being when they are in a fear mode, and they always have to eat. In rising markets, financial stocks often lead the parade. But still the question arises, which ones? There is lots of analyst advice available, but then you are taking a risk. Or you could head for the hills, go completely into cash, and wait for good times to return. You won't make much money, but you won't lose anything either. You could buy insurance, as we have discussed earlier, but depending upon your fear level, that might not be enough. Anytime we are faced with the decision of which stocks to buy in uncertain times, fear can make all of us uncertain of our decisions.

You could always be a buy-and-hold investor, but that isn't likely to work either, as you could lose a lot of money in the process. Markets can and do go to sleep for years, as they wait for geopolitical events to sort themselves out. One of the reasons I have become interested in thematic investing is that it allows an investor to concentrate on a subject whose outcome might be reasonably predictable. Yes, it is possible that diets in emerging markets might deteriorate in the face of some event, but once people are well fed, they don't like going back to eating poorly. They will make different kinds of trade-offs than they might have before in order to keep food on the table. Or, if there is a major demographic shift in a country, it will be years before another shift occurs, so you can predict fairly accurately how many people are going to do specific things in their lives, and then invest accordingly.

Look at Argentina. In 1900, it was one of the ten richest nations on earth, endowed with fertile soil, oil, grain, beef, and rich mineral resources. But decades of fiscal mismanagement and class warfare had reduced Argentina to pauperism by 2000, and in 2002 the nation defaulted on $75 billion in international bonds. Poverty doubled from 27 percent to 54 percent, and millions of Argentines had their life savings wiped out. Despite all this, the nation maintained its traditional diet of expensive beef, which could have been exported to help pay down the debt, and the government offered twenty-five cents on the dollar to bondholders. By 2004, the bondholders had largely accepted the government's deal, and the Argentine economy had begun to grow. During all that time, the diet never changed. If it had, Argentines would have brought down their government.

Now let's look at greed. There are two ways to see greed. One is that it is the opposite of fear, the desire for more: Alan Greenspan's "irrational exuberance," the feeling that nothing you can do is wrong and that every decision you are going to make is going to be right. That has happened, to be sure. Just look at the Internet and telecom bubbles of the 1990s and the real estate bubble that is now deflating, or the emerging market carry trade investment bubble of the past few years. All of those bubbles enriched those who discerned the trend early and cost the laggards a fortune when the bubble burst. Another way to look at greed is as a subset of fear. Greed is the desire to have more than your fair share, however you define fair share. Greed is pathological, while fear can often be constructive and prevent you from getting into trouble. Greed is really the fear that someone else will get more than you, deprive you of your ability to get more than they have. I don't know how to overcome greed, but I do know that when you sense it coming on—when you begin dreaming about how much your investments might make if they can only go up a couple of additional percentage points—well, that's the time to exit an investment, because your decision-making skills have collapsed. If you have to choose between getting in late or getting out early, always get out early, because while you lose a bit on the upside by getting into an investment late, you never lose by getting out early.

CHAPTER 8

TOO MUCH *versus* TOO LITTLE INFORMATION

In many respects, this ought to be the first binary, because knowledge is power. When things don't make sense, it's either because you don't have enough information or because you have too much. If you have a lot of information and you still can't figure out what's going on in a market, it's a safe bet than no one else can either.

A couple of years into my career at Morgan, I was transferred from Madrid, where I'd begun my career, and sent to Mexico City, where I was one of the first people from Morgan to work. In Mexico the authorities gave us minimal access to a market that was booming with petrodollars but beset by protectionism and poor economic policies. It was a recipe for economic disaster, and anyone with any sense could see that there was a bubble building, one that would burst and take anyone and anything invested in pesos down with it.

It was exactly the kind of market where fortunes are both made and lost, one where the information flow is at once huge and contradictory, fueled as much by rumor and speculation as the truth. The numbers were especially hard to believe. Companies could borrow all the money they wanted, and banks were driving down their own spreads and charging next to nothing—all for the dubious privilege of becoming the lead banker on deals.

When things don't make sense to you—because of too much or too little information—you have two choices: short the market (that is, buy options on the expectation that the market or your stocks will go down) or get out altogether. In Mexico, I chose a variety of shorting: I went into the local market to borrow pesos from Citibank (remember, I was working

for Morgan then), sold them for dollars, and then sold dollar-forward contracts back to the Bank of America, picking up 2,000 basis points (20 percent) of arbitrage along the way, with American banks on either side of
the trade. Done within the authorized limits set by Morgan, we made a lot
of money. I had found a waterfall. (I admit this is not a strategy the average investor can pull off. But I'm talking here about *how to think,* not one
specific financial play.)

We were making so much that I grew concerned. Making money can't
be this easy, I thought. And if it was, why didn't anyone else figure out
what we were doing and jump in? When you find what looks like a waterfall, you always have to ask: Why me? Is it a mirage? Is it illegal? When
will it run out?

I turned to my boss with these questions, and Morgan put me on a
plane to New York for a conversation with Dennis Weatherstone, the head
of foreign exchange and later Morgan's president and chairman. His
words were simple: if that's the way the market was behaving, it was clear
that the Mexicans were expecting a peso devaluation. The Mexicans were,
in fact, losing faith in their own economy. Those who understood that and
put their bucket into forward peso contracts protected their fortunes, and
those who didn't lost their money. Eventually, it all came to an end on September 1, 1982, when the Mexican government nationalized the banks. I
showed up at my office that day and found a tank barring my path. As the
economy collapsed, Mexico's president found it more convenient to
blame the banking system than to accept responsibility for his mismanagement. For a few days it was pretty touch and go, but cooler heads prevailed and we reopened. A decade of turmoil followed, climaxing when
the U.S. Treasury bailed out Mexico in 1995.

Too much information can often muddle your decision making. If you
can't make sense out of a glut of information, look for something simpler.
Almost every day, when you pick up the newspaper, there is at least one
article about China's growing economic strength, which is enticing for investors. But if you've been doing your reading, you've also noticed all the
articles telling you how risky it is to invest in Chinese equities. What do
you do? You could pick around the edges and invest in the companies
supplying China with infrastructure, or you could invest in consumer

product companies selling in China, but neither approach gets you to the heart of the matter. You might buy the Walt Disney Company, which has just opened a new theme park in Hong Kong, but that's only a single stream of revenue for a very large company, and if you've read some Disney annual reports and some brokerage commentary, you know that Disney has had mixed success with foreign theme parks. So what do you do? Open your mind and ask yourself, What do I know about the Chinese?

One thing I know is that they are inveterate gamblers, even though gambling is banned in China. So the Chinese go to Macao, a tiny Portuguese colony that was returned to China in the 1990s that allows gambling. Macao's wagering is now almost as large as the "handle"—the amount wagered—in Las Vegas. In 2006 the two gambling hubs equaled each other in money wagered, and in 2007, Macao surpassed Las Vegas as the gambling capital of the world. All of the major U.S. casino companies know this, and nearly all of them are building casinos in Macao to take advantage of China's gambling habit. They have placed their buckets under the waterfall of Macao. They don't need to know anything about China's five-year plans or its plans to invest in infrastructure or energy or anything else. If Macao is a good enough investment for Steve Wynn or Sheldon Adelson, two of the most successful investors in Las Vegas real estate, it may be a safe bet for individual investors as well. All you have to learn is which of the casino companies is planning to open in Macao, because their revenues will be impacted the most by that investment. That is not a lot of information, and it is all publicly available.

One way to deal with information is to learn the approach advocated by Colonel John Boyd, a famous fighter pilot, but more important, a famous teacher of strategy and tactics whose decision analysis process is now standard procedure for the U.S. Marines. Boyd invented something he called the "OODA loop." The initials stand for *observe, orient, decide* and *act*. Boyd says that during the Korean War, the "kill ratio" between American fighter pilots in Sabre jets and the North Koreans and Russians in MiGs began to change in favor of the Americans after they learned the OODA process. Boyd told his pilots that if they observed their opponents for a while, they could begin to figure out their tendencies and then figure out how to take advantage of them. In aerial combat, that meant learning how to make tighter turns to get in behind their opponents, so that their guns and rockets came into play and not those of their opponents. To do that, though, they had to go through a complete cycle of observing, orienting, deciding, and acting, at a rate more rapid than their opponents, who might have been doing exactly the same thing. Boyd believed that there were doctrinal differences that could be exploited to help pilots make faster decisions, the differences in the way the North Koreans were taught and the way Americans learned aerial combat. What does that mean? It is the question of how you approach information. How much information do you need to know before you can make a decision that has a high probability of being correct, to buy or to sell? That may be the single most critical question that you will have to solve, because the more information you need, the slower you are going to be getting into a market—and the slower you are probably going to be getting out. While getting in late means you might pay a slight penalty in not realizing all of the potential gains of a rising market, getting out late is almost always costly.

So how much information do you need? Part of the answer is based on individual behavior, which develops over years. Are you quick or slow, impulsive or deliberate, in your approach to problems? These are character traits that you might change over time, but a simpler way is to learn how to organize information more deliberately. I observe by listening to my clients and how they are investing. I orient myself by reading everything thoroughly, talking with experts, and getting their opinions. Much of what we take to be original thinking is really received wisdom, and the trick is to synthesize what you have learned on your own with what smart people tell you. That synthesis, which you have been doing since college—remember "compare and contrast" papers in history and literature?—will provide you with an orientation, a personal take on what you have learned, and the foundation for making decisions.

Once you have properly oriented yourself to a problem, the next step is making the decision to act. That's the critical step. Are you going to buy, sell, hold, or ignore the opportunity altogether and look for some other opportunity? Decision making has two components: the decision itself and the speed with which you make it. In investing, many decisions are time-sensitive. Markets are in constant motion, and you have to make decisions quickly to get the greatest gains, especially if you are gong to make short-term investments. With long-term thematic investments, quickness is not as necessary, which is another reason I favor thematic investing. Quickness ultimately requires the nerves and calm of a fighter pilot, and few of us have those.

How do you know when you are right? You don't, so you have to practice. Do you remember what I said about saving back at the beginning of the book? Learn to save and accumulate money, and while you are doing that, begin to make observations and orient yourself toward decision making. Make hypothetical decisions and follow them in the market, being totally honest with yourself at all times. Unlike golf among friends, there are no gimmes in investing. Once you have made enough practice decisions—pick a theme, pretend to make some investments within that theme, do some research to validate your opinions, and then follow your investments closely—you will begin to gain a sense of whether or not you are right or wrong, and then keep doing it until your confidence level rises to the point where you are not afraid to act. And then act. Start small, because you are still going to need more courage than you think. Action is the willingness to trust your observations. In life, as in investing, taking action is not always easy, even when you have a method to help you along. But if you don't learn not only to take action when it is appropriate but also to do it with alacrity, you cannot hope to do well as an investor.

CHAPTER 9

PRESERVATION *versus* GROWTH

Aside from misreading *when* to employ capital, investors often also miss out on the *how.* The following chart tracks three trends: the rise and fall of yield rates for 3-month CDs and for 10-year Treasury bills (an indicator of the urge to preserve money) against the movement of the S&P 500 index since 1980.

Interest rates peaked just before 1980—at more than 18 percent!—yet the stock market didn't take off until about 1992. That fourteen-year gap spells opportunity if you can see it, and it provides a perfect illustration of preservation versus growth.

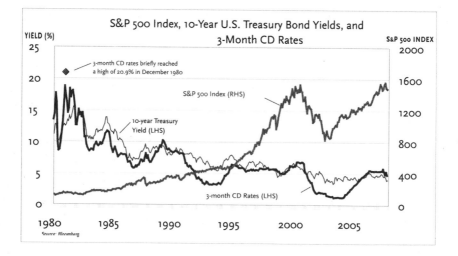

From 1992 to 2002, investors made money in both growth and preservation strategies, as bond investors used the carry trade to profit from falling rates and stock investors enjoyed rising markets. The same thing was true in 2003 and 2004, only you had to have new money to put into the market at that point, and you couldn't merely be recovering from the more than 40 percent drop in the S&P 500. It is possible to make money in both up and down markets, to prosper with preservation strategies, such as investing in the carry trade when short rates are dropping faster than long rates, and to prosper in growth strategies, such as finding a new set of markets ready to take off. If you truly want to prosper, you can't afford to make money only in the years when the stock market is rising. You have to look for investments that will give you a positive return even when equity markets are going nowhere or are in decline.

First, you need to look beyond stocks. The vast majority of Americans and a growing number of international investors allocate the largest percentage of their portfolios to equities. They have been schooled by an equity-obsessed media and years of study showing that over long periods of time, equities provide the best return. Though equities were once presumed to be dead in the water, I won't dispute that, but as we saw earlier, there are times when equities hit the doldrums, and in those periods you need to find something else to do with your money. The question is, do you work to preserve what you have, or do you attempt to make your money grow? Most investors would opt for a preservation strategy, retreating into the safety of bonds or cash. Even there, it is possible to make money.

A decade ago, your choices in bonds would have been high-grade U.S. corporates, high-yield U.S. corporates—a euphemism for junk bonds— or U.S. Treasuries. But just as the equity markets have globalized, so too have the bond markets. Bonds are now issued not only in the major trading currencies—the euro, the Japanese yen, and the British pound—but in other currencies, such as the Thai baht and the Malaysian ringgit. There are large and growing markets for these bonds, making them almost as liquid as their better-known counterparts.

The key to a bond strategy is not much different from that of a stock strategy, except that with bonds, you have better information. Bonds are classified according to their quality by three rating agencies: Standard & Poor's, Moody's, and Fitch. Their rating systems differ somewhat, but it is rare when one of the agencies rates a bond highly and another does not. However, what all of the rating agencies have in common is a bias toward U.S. Treasuries. Because the U.S. economy is the largest and strongest in the world, conventional wisdom has overtaken the bond market, that U.S. Treasuries are the safest investment, the benchmark against which all other investments are measured, since it is assumed that the default risk of the U.S. government is zero. The rating agencies accord a near-zero risk to bonds issued by Japan, the European Union, and Great Britain, but from there, the risk levels begin to rise and the ratings begin to fall. Part of the risk profile—a large part for some countries—is past history, so nations such as Mexico, Brazil, and Argentina, which have all either defaulted on their bonds or come perilously close to doing so, are accorded a higher risk profile and a lower rating even as their economies are humming. The rating is based upon a presumption that something is bound to go wrong and that the rating must reflect that notional risk, even if it is not there at present.

It is in that built-in bias that the opportunity for a growth strategy lurks. Many nations that have in the past exhibited poor fiscal judgment have, over the past twenty years, begun to reform, to improve the transparency of governance, and to get their fiscal houses in order. Some, such as Brazil and Mexico, have developed enormous current account surpluses. That is, they have vastly more money in their treasuries than they need in order to service the interest on their bonds. By definition, those surpluses ought to gain them an upgrade from the rating agencies, because they are a de facto guarantee against default, but the rating agencies have long memories and have seen such surpluses evaporate as a new government comes to power, or a crisis in commodity prices occurs, or any one of a dozen other calamities befalls the country in question. On Wall Street, you often hear the words "This time it's different" whenever we are in the middle of a boom. We heard that in the late 1990s, as Internet stocks and their investors marched on like lemmings, steadily upward with no end in sight. We heard it again between 2002 and 2006, as bond interest rates around the world fell in unison. Each time the words

"This time it's different" echoed down Wall Street, the smartest investors headed for the exits. It is never different. Every time investors become overly fond of an asset class, too much money pours in and the class crashes, as Internet stocks did in 2000 and as bonds did in mid-2006. But in mid-2006, it really was different. As global bond values crashed, smart investors looked at small nations and discovered that they were wrong for dumping their bonds universally. For example, during the mid-2006 bond debacle, Brazil used the opportunity to pay off its debt to the International Monetary Fund, using a bit of its current account surplus while continuing to hold the line on its economic policies. This strategy so improved Brazil's fiscal position that smart traders began to notice, and the value of the bonds began to recover. The same was true with India, Mexico, and half a dozen other nations where the rating agencies had missed the march down the path of reform. The smart investors who did notice, however, were able to make huge profits by buying when the bonds tumbled and then selling as they recovered.

Closer to home, the same thing happened with the bonds of General Motors. GM has long had a reputation as being one of the most astute money managers on Wall Street (the joke runs that if GM made cars as well as it made money, it would again dominate the auto world). In the summer of 2004, near the bottom of interest rates in the United States, General Motors went to Wall Street and borrowed several billion dollars for 30 years at a coupon rate of 8.375 percent, a nice return for investors when cash was paying 2 percent and U.S. Treasury bonds weren't paying much more. The following spring, all of the rating agencies, distressed by GM's poor sales and growing pension liabilities, downgraded GM's bonds to junk status. The 30-year 8.375 percent bonds shot up overnight, yielding more than 12 percent as nervous investors dumped the bonds en masse. But those who had done a little research noticed that GM's pension liabilities came in two forms—those it had to pay immediately, which the bond borrowing was meant to cover, and a much larger contingent liability that could be paid out over decades, from current accounts, should GM return to profitability. Digging a little deeper, smart investors discovered that the demographics for GM would soon improve, as the number of GM workers covered by contingent health care costs should begin to diminish around 2010. Moreover, GM and the United Auto Workers were beginning serious negotiations to drive those future health care costs down.

If you had assessed all of that information and ignored the conventional wisdom that GM was headed for the scrap heap, you would have bought the 8.375 percent bonds and waited. Sure enough, by September 2005 the rest of the world came to the same conclusion, and the bonds returned very close to 8.375 percent. In the interval you would have been more than 40 percent ahead when you sold them, in addition to the accrued interest you would have collected. Furthermore, if you had then taken your bond profits and purchased GM stock in the late autumn of 2005 and sold during the summer of 2006, you would have been ahead by another 46 percent. In other words, with a little courage, a little research, and a willingness to counter the conventional wisdom, it was possible to almost double your money on what appeared to be, on the surface, a troubled company that everyone else believed was doomed.

How often do such opportunities come along? Surprisingly, nearly every day. The mantra of Wall Street theorists is that prices reflect perfect information. Especially in the age of the Internet and the blogosphere, some hold that every bit of knowable information about a security is instantly known by everyone. Well, guess what? It isn't true, and it never has been. Little black holes of information always open up. Situations change, and so Wall Street's perception changes, sometimes rightly, but just as often wrongly. Conventional wisdom sets in, and that perception remains until an event of sufficient importance dislodges it—in Brazil's case, it was the nation's decision to pay off its IMF debt that made investors sit up and take notice; in GM's case, it took a sufficient number of bond traders rushing in after the ratings downgrade to drive home the point that the rating agencies might have overreacted. Between the time when you find an opportunity and when other investors do is, of course, the best time to make money, because sooner or later, Wall Street does catch up and process new information.

When use of the Internet as a research and communications tool became ubiquitous, many assumed that those little information black holes would disappear. What they did not count on was that at the same time,

Wall Street firms were beginning to make significant cuts in their analyst coverage of many companies. Most analysts made their money serving the large institutions, and as those institutions—pension funds, insurance companies, and large endowments—began to concentrate their holdings among the largest and most steadily profitable companies, analyst coverage of smaller and medium-sized companies began to shrink. The bursting of the Internet and telecom bubbles caused further shrinkage in analyst coverage, while the growth of electronic trading, ironically, caused further shrinkage, as investors began to subscribe to more independent research at the expense of house research from the large brokerages. All of these factors have combined to deemphasize original, thoughtful research at a time when it is sorely needed. Investors are more and more on their own. But the decline of coverage also helps to create more opportunity, because investors cannot look everywhere. Wall Street no longer has perfect knowledge—it never did—and growth opportunities have emerged.

Investing in GM at the right time would have helped you double your money in about fifteen months, but do you really need to do that? Well, there's nothing like doubling to boost your long-term batting average, because you aren't going to do so well on every investment. Remember: ten is nothing more than fourteen ahead and four back. It is not always three plus seven or nine plus one. Also, remember that your purpose in investing is not to become a braggart at the country club. You are investing to secure retirement, or to supplement your income when your child's college tuition comes up, or for any of a thousand other legitimate reasons. So you want to hit the double when you can, but otherwise, you want to stay a couple of points ahead of the rate of inflation plus the interest rate on 30-year bonds. If bonds are running at 5 percent and inflation is at 3 percent, you are shooting for 9 percent or 10 percent. But if bonds are at 3 percent and inflation is zero, as it was just four years ago, a 5 percent or 6 percent return will be just fine.

Often, the best time to make money is when inflation is low and interest rates are also low. At that point, the spread between the best investments and the worst ones is wide at first, though it will begin to narrow. In the absence of high interest rates and inflation, investor tolerance for risk rises. People see that wide spread as a protective margin of error and believe that they can profit from it. This is exactly what happened between 2002 and mid-2004. Part of the problem with the carry trade was that as the spread between quality bonds and junk bonds began to fall and as the default rate on junk bonds reached historic lows, risk seemed to disappear. At that moment, investors could buy the worst-rated asset for little more risk premium than the best-rated assets. Investors flooded into junk bonds and into the bonds of previously low-rated nations such as the Philippines. At the same time, the perception of the risk in equities, as measured by the VIX, an index of volatility in the stock market, was also diving to historic lows. This gave investors a false sense of security, and just as the end of the carry trade has burned bond investors, some event may come along and do the same to investors in stocks. How carefully you pay attention to this possibility will determine whether you make out or get burned.

Let's recapitulate. You want to preserve capital at all times, and you want to make it grow whenever the opportunity arises. You want to stay ahead of the combination of interest rates and inflation as a minimum; when that combination gets too high, as it began to in late 2006, then you want to remain in a preservation mode, because it becomes more difficult to earn the kind of return you want without taking on unneeded risk. But since you want to keep moving forward, you want some return, all you need to do is look for something you know will give you the best return for the least risk. If Treasuries are paying 5 percent, that might not be so bad, if you can move back into high-quality equities and get a significant bounce as times improve, and then into slightly riskier assets, such as emerging market equities. If each year your investments remain in positive territory on an absolute basis, over time you will do well enough so that your total investment will rise quite significantly.

CHAPTER 10

DIRECTIONAL *versus* NONDIRECTIONAL

I've never been a huge fan of reliance on benchmarking. It is a form of investing that is meant to protect money managers from their mistakes. Benchmarking ensures them that they will remain close to some arbitrary average performance based on their own personal investment style. These averages ensure that most fund managers will collect their year-end bonuses, but they do little for the investor, because they allow—even encourage—mediocrity. But there are some useful tools that have come out of asset allocation modeling, and one of them is asset correlation. By charting many different investment classes over long periods of time, it is possible to say with some authority that when certain investments are going up, certain others will go down. The most obvious of these is the relationship between stocks and bonds. Conversely, some investments historically rise at the same time, such as real estate and stocks. Traditionally, when a portfolio rises in value, a flush investor may be willing to invest in an expansion of his or her lifestyle, which often means a bigger house. Since interest rates are often falling at the same time, an investing boom and a real estate boom can be concurrent. This correlation and noncorrelation of investment classes is at the heart of deciding whether to invest in directional or nondirectional strategies. Directional strategies—investing on the presumption that your investment class is headed in one direction, up—make sense when the economy is growing and all signs point to a continuation of growth. But when the investment outcome is uncertain or headed into negative territory, you ought to consider nondirectional investing, looking for investments that don't correlate or have negative correlations to each other. This strategy puts you into the realm of hedge fund managers. Hedge funds are basically nondirectional investments designed to take advantage of the indecision of markets. Once upon a time, you needed to be a millionaire in order to be qualified to invest in hedge funds—they are loosely regulated, and it is possible for investors to lose all of their money quickly if a manager's strategy goes awry. Managers don't want lawsuits from investors who don't understand this risk, and neither does the SEC, so only wealthy investors are allowed to use hedge funds as investment vehicles. But increasingly, institutional investors such as universities and mutual funds have placed a portion of their money with hedge fund mangers, to their customers' benefit.

While many readers of this book cannot invest in hedge funds directly, it is worthwhile to study hedge fund strategies, as they provide useful insights into what some call "thematic investing," which is just what it implies—investing according to a theme, such as mergers and acquisitions or long/short investing. These are different from the themes I wrote about earlier, such as demographics, energy, and the path of reform. My themes are directly based on observable events in the real world, while hedge fund themes are based upon market events and are really not much different from mutual fund themes, which are focused on industrial sectors or investing styles, such as value investing or growth investing. Hedge funds look for situations where those informational black holes I wrote about earlier might arise. For example, in 2004, the M&A market began to heat up as the stock prices of many companies continued to fall or remain stagnant, even in the face of rising profits and retained earnings. As I write this, U.S. corporations have piled up almost $1 trillion in money that has not been spent on expansion or returned to the shareholders in the form of dividends or share buybacks. Several noted strategists on Wall Street refuse to believe that this situation can persist and have advised their clients to buy the shares of companies with lots of cash, on the assumption that that cash will eventually be distributed. Many hedge fund managers believe that the cash holdup will persist and that the cash will set off a furious round of mergers and acquisitions. One company will take over another and use the takeover victim's available cash to pay for the cost of the acquisition. Between 2004 and early 2006, this strategy worked well for hedge fund managers, but then it stopped working, as M&A activity ground almost to a halt. What had happened? First, most of the good acquisitions had already been made. More important, managers with a lot of cash in the till began to take on corporate debt. Their thinking was that interest rates were low and set to rise, so why not borrow now and use a company's cash to hedge against uncertainty in the future?

Another style of hedge fund management is event-driven. If you can figure out what is going to happen to a particular sector or company, you can get in front of the event and profit from it as it happens. Over the summer of 2006, if you had been paying attention to the news, you might have noticed that Congress was getting more serious about corporate pension reform. If a law is passed, that's an event, because it forces companies to change the way they do business. In fact, when the law was ultimately changed, it was a boon to companies that already had their pension plans in shape and harmful to those that did not, because the new law forces those companies to allocate enough money to bring their pension plans up to standard within seven years. Those companies will have to do a lot of borrowing or divert a lot of corporate cash into pension coffers. Both solutions will change the companies' financial statuses, making them less desirable from an investment standpoint in the short run. If you are an event-driven hedge fund manager who is focusing on pensions, you might well be shorting some of these stocks in anticipation that they will fall, or you might be waiting for them to fall as an opportunity to purchase in the future. Another set of events is geopolitical. We see the effect of geopolitical events on oil prices every day, as unrest in the Middle East drives up energy prices, while the semblance of peace allows them to drift lower. By now, smart event-driven hedge fund managers know approximately how much energy prices will rise or fall from a given event, and they can invest accordingly in the energy futures market.

Another hedge fund style that helps an investor get around the correlation problem is called long/short investing. Within any industrial sector, such as chemicals, oil, or computer software, some companies are doing very well and others are doing poorly. If you amass knowledge of the sector, it is possible to go long on the good companies and profit as their shares rise and to short the poor companies, on the assumption that they will be further punished by investors for their poor performance. Your responsibility here, should you decide to invest on a long/short basis, is to watch your basket of stocks carefully. At a certain point in time, your longs will run out of upward momentum, since everyone else will have recognized their potential. At that point, you have to get out of those stocks, or short them, on the assumption that they have no place to go but down. Likewise, when the stocks at the bottom, which you have been shorting, begin to nudge upward, it is time to end to your short positions and go long. If you want to use long/short as an investment method effectively, you have to watch both sides and be prepared to switch tactics rapidly. This is where decision-making skill becomes paramount.

All of these nondirectional strategies have their moments, and each can be ended abruptly as conditions in the economy, interest rates, or world events change the circumstances surrounding the strategy. Realize that there are now more than seven thousand hedge fund managers, all attempting to make money off a limited number of nondirectional strategies, and you can begin to see that these strategies may have diminished payoffs. The hedge fund managers should worry, but not you. They are looking for huge gains. You are looking for strategies that will take a small gain and add to it. So, for example, if the combination of inflation and 30-year Treasuries is 8 percent, all you need to do is get 4 percent out of a nondirectional strategy to remain ahead as you are earning 5 percent from your cash. Nine is better than eight, and if you can hold to nine while eight becomes seven or six, you will do well over time.

Of all the nondirectional investments you can make, real estate is, paradoxically, both the hardest and the easiest one from which you can make additional profit. Real estate prices are influenced by national events, such as the rise and fall of interest rates and employment rates, and they are also influenced by local events, such as the opening of a large factory or a casino. Even in the midst of a national downturn, some cities are more recession-resistant than others, and in an upturn, some cities will trail a national recovery by months or even years. Because it is difficult to manage real estate from afar—it really pays to look at the property in which you are going to invest, to look at the neighborhood, and to take a close look at the local economy—many investors have backed off from real estate. According to the 2006 Capgemini/Merrill Lynch World Wealth Report, the number of high-net-worth investors putting money into real estate has dropped by about a percentage point a year for the past five years. It now stands at about 12 percent. But this number is deceptive. Many investors, realizing that real estate investing is attractive but also difficult, have done what legions of stock investors did before them: they have bought mutual funds. These real estate funds, called "real estate investment trusts," or REITs, have existed for decades. Unlike mutual funds, which may hold on to cash, REITs are designed by law to pay out all of their profits every year. If the national real estate market is doing well, REIT profits can be large. When the market is doing poorly, REITs depend upon the real estate leasing cycle to get by. A well-managed REIT will have only a small percentage of its leases come up for renewal each year, so that if vacancy rates rise, as they do in an economic downturn, the impact on the REIT, and on the investor, is decreased. Best of all, most REITs are publicly traded, so they have high liquidity, should you decide that you want to move into another asset class if a better opportunity turns up.

Another way to partake in real estate is through a private equity fund. The principal is the same as with a REIT. A professional manager buys a portfolio of properties with the money invested by a group of partners and pays out a steady stream of income based upon the rents. The investor also gets a tax advantage through his or her share of the depreciation on the properties. The difference is that private equity deals are illiquid. Once your money is invested, it is locked up for the life of the deal, usually ten years. Moreover, you have to trust your manager, often difficult to do in these troubled investing times. Nevertheless, many people go the private equity route, and it is not unlikely that over time, a trading market will develop in private equity partnerships, providing partners who want the option of getting out with a way to liquidate without huge penalties.

To sum up: In good times, most investors prefer to be directional. They can acquire enough information about the stock or bond they want to back. There is typically enough evidence from the economy and other sources that the market in general and their investment in particular will go up. In hard times, or in times where the market has lost direction, investors have to choose between remaining on the sidelines and looking at investments that do not correlate well with stocks. Bonds are the first choice among nondirectional investors, since they tend to rise when stocks fall, but other nondirectional asset classes, such as hedge funds and real estate, are also growing viable. Another way to escape the long-only trap is international diversification: go long, but go long somewhere else. That is covered in the next section.

PART III

A CHANGING MARKET

This section is called "A Changing Market," and what that really denotes is global realignment. When I began in this business several decades ago, there were only a handful of meaningful stock markets around the world. The United States accounted for almost three-quarters of the volume of trading by value, and about half of it by volume. London and Tokyo were meaningful stock markets, with active, continuous trading. There were a handful of smaller markets that acted in a similar fashion, such as Hong Kong, but most stock markets that did exist—there were perhaps fifty—followed the French model. There, stock prices were fixed by a handful of brokers in the morning, based upon the previous day's demand and any news about a company that had come in overnight, and then the brokers took orders and went out to a long lunch. If the orders were above expectations, they refixed prices upward. If they were below expected demand, they refixed prices downward. Then they waited for the afternoon's response. Then they went to dinner at one of the restaurants in the neighborhood around the Bourse, the name of their market, and went home to their wives or mistresses. It was quiet, polite, a completely closed game.

ELECTRONIC MARKETS

Beginning around 1990, the markets began to change. The U.S. markets had gone through an electronic revolution following the meltdown of 1987, and trading and settlement in American markets were greatly sped up and made more accurate as a result. No longer did the market have to depend upon little slips of paper handed off to clerks. Now the specialists who controlled trading on the New York Stock Exchange or the brokers who did their trading on the American or the NASDAQ could type in a stock ticker symbol and have a computer match buy and sell orders, even settle the account—move money from one account to another—at the same time. In order to allow for heavy volume, the system still permitted two days for settlement, but that was a vast improvement over the week that it had taken previously. Many of the companies that developed the software for automating trading on U.S. exchanges saw a similar opportunity in overseas exchanges, and so such automation began to spread.

For the American exchanges, the selling proposition associated with automation was order execution and volume. For small foreign exchanges, it turned out to be liquidity. Setting stock prices only twice a day impaired trading, affecting the liquidity not of stocks already on the market but of possible new issues. Besides its initial capital, why does a company go public? What does it get once the initial public offering is done and the cash raised is safely in the corporate coffers? The answer, generally, is a lot more scrutiny and a lot of shareholders who will send the share price plummeting at the least sign of underperformance. Why bother, then? The answer is liquidity. If you want to raise more money, your open, transparent performance means that you are no longer at the mercy of a small number of banks. In smaller nations, where an oligarchy might own or control much of the nation's capital, an open market is a shortcut to prosperity. An open market allows a company to be judged on its merits, not on the opinions or prejudices of a small coterie of powerful people.

If a company wants to have a chance to drive up its value, it has to be able to withstand public exposure. The good deeds and valiant efforts of a chief executive officer can be cheered on, rewarded. All that is good about companies—and all that is bad—shows up in the stock market, a daily vote of confidence or no confidence in each and every company listed. Liquidity improves the voting process. That turned out to be an almost irresistible lure, and in short order, between 1988 and

1992 or so, more than 130 nations launched modern electronic markets. The International Organization of Securities Clearing Organizations (IOSCO) morphed from a minor study group in Montreal that researched global markets into a supervisory body overseeing worldwide rules for securities trading. These included faster settlement rules, common laws for securities transactions, rules about transparency in dealing with customers, resolution mechanisms, and recommendations that have opened markets to global trading. At the same time that smarter, faster markets were opening, many nations began to make their currencies freely convertible in order to attract foreign investment for development. Convertibility made it possible for foreign investors to buy in and cash out of a market at the same speed as local investors without having to establish a source of local capital.

DERIVATIVES

A second significant change in markets that took place over the past decade or so is the growth of derivative markets, especially futures. With a derivative, you do not own a stock, but rather a bet on what might happen to it within a given period of time. Derivatives began with the advent of the futures markets in the late nineteenth century as a mechanism for dealing with the price of commodities in between the time they were harvested and the time they were handed over to a processor. As telegraph lines and then telephones linked even the remotest farms to the big cities, farmers have relied upon the futures markets to make decisions about when to bring their crops to market. If you know that the current price of a bushel of wheat at the loading dock in Minneapolis is $5 but traders believe that in thirty days enough additional wheat will be on the market to drive the price down to $4, you sell your current wheat today. If, on the other hand, the future price is high enough to pay for the cost of keeping your wheat off the market for a while, you sell a "future" on the wheat—a promise to deliver—for a later date. Futures trading creates more orderly markets by helping regulate supply and demand. Futures also provide an interesting barometer on conventional wisdom. If, for example, the price of oil is $70 a barrel and the futures market says that it is going to be $60 a barrel a year from now, that ought to be a signal for potential investors to figure out why the traders believe the price will drop so dramatically. And here is where it gets interesting, because the people who are regular traders in a commodity or in some other derivative, such as Dow Jones Industrial Average futures, often get it wrong. Predicting the future is difficult work, and most of the so-called experts are right only about half the time—which means that they also get it wrong half the time. That creates windows of opportunity that can allow you to boost your own percentage. Since a growing number of securities and commodities now have futures attached to them, the window of opportunity is immense.

Indeed, as modern, up-to-date stock markets have spread around the world—and the knowledge of securities transactions with them—the variety of futures contracts available has increased dramatically and the number of contracts has increased exponentially. There are now many more futures contracts in oil traded than actual barrels of oil to be delivered, many more currency contracts and contracts for Treasury futures than real T-bills. You can get a feel for how the larger investing community anticipates the future and adjust your own portfolio accordingly if you observe the markets actively, read the newspapers, and ensure that your own biases are not skewing your perspective.

While futures are supposed to create more orderly markets, sometimes they can add disorder in the marketplace. Another name for disorder is volatility, and another name for volatility is uncertainty, and when uncertainty increases in the market, there is a natural tendency to correct it. The problem is that futures contracts have fixed expiration dates, so often, as the expiration date approaches, a flurry of buying and selling erupts that has absolutely nothing to do with the real world but rather with traders attempting to cover potential losses. These expiration dates, called "witching hours," can cause sharp spikes in volatility, bend entire markets. In October 1987, a so-called triple witching hour occurred when 1-month, 3-month, and 6-month contracts all expired on the same day, and computerized trading programs designed to give traders an edge dumped billions of shares onto the market, resulting in the largest one-day plunge in American stock market history by both value and volume. Once investors realized that there was no underlying economic reason for the fall, stocks recovered and resumed their upward track and the stock exchanges put in place new rules to prevent a similar drop from happening in the future. That is not to say that the markets will never suffer another catastrophic loss, just that it probably won't come from the rapid computerized trading of futures.

New Products

The globalization of trading and the growth of derivatives has been accompanied by yet a third phenomenon: a blizzard of new products available to investors, some of which, like ETFs and indexes, have a long shelf life, while others, such as capital markets investments, do not. Almost every major broker and investment bank now runs a capital markets desk, which puts together specialized investment products for customers that are some combination of a cash or currency transaction with some other form of security to provide a slightly greater probability of upside gain while minimizing downside risk. These transactions were conceived only for sophisticated investors, but then, so were mutual funds at one time. In the financial markets, as in many consumer markets, the profit lure causes someone to figure out how to productize a complicated instrument for the masses, leading to an increase in trading volume and more commissions. One of the ironies of Wall Street is that while commission spreads—what a firm charges for a transaction versus its expenses for executing it—have narrowed over the past two decades, firms on the street are making more money than ever and paying ever more generous bonuses. While the money supply has grown at a decent rate, the turnover of that money, via the creation of a growing number of trading vehicles, like the old joke, makes up in volume what it gives away in price.

. . .

In the coming chapters, I will cover a number of subjects that have been affected by the development of new markets. Investors not only have to grow smarter about what they know, they have to grow smarter about what they don't know, if they are going to succeed in markets where so many do poorly.

CHAPTER 11

RISING INTEREST *versus* FALLING INTEREST RATES   RATES

We've said this before: when interest rates rise, stocks fall, and vice versa. For two decades, there has been a fairly close correlation between the two, simply because investors have operated in a stable environment where risks are well known. Indeed, over that twenty-year period, Americans lived in an environment of falling interest rates. After the oil shocks of the 1970s, Federal Reserve chairman Paul Volcker pushed interest rates into the stratosphere to break the back of inflation, and from that moment through 2004, rates were allowed to fall. For the first several years of declines, there was no rise in the stock markets, as one might have expected, because investors were beaten down from a decade of watching their portfolios stagnate. They failed to recognize good news when they saw it.

But one small group of investors not only recognized the opportunities of a falling-interest-rate environment; they also became billionaires in the process. Mike Milken, T. Boone Pickens, Henry Kravis, and a group of Wall Street investment bankers began to realize around 1984 that because stocks had failed to respond to falling interest rates, they were probably undervalued. A closer look at many of the companies that appeared undervalued showed just how poorly Wall Street understood these companies. Many of them either had huge amounts of cash on their balance sheets, cash acquired during the inflation-ridden 1970s as a hedge against even higher future prices, or, if they were companies that had grown by takeover, had undervalued corporate assets. Some of them had both. Milken, Pickens, and the rest realized that if you could put together some capital of your own, you could launch a takeover bid for an undervalued company and use either the existing cash in the till or sell off an under-valued division to pay for the entire cost of the takeover.

Once the takeover boom of the mid-1980s was launched, Wall Street was forced to take another look at stocks. A boom began that, with a few hiccups along the way, lasted until 2000. All that time, as stocks rose, interest rates declined, if for no other reason that the demand for debt financing was in decline. In a rising stock market, entrepreneurs discov-ered a financing vehicle that could make them rich overnight. Debt, on the other hand, needed to be repaid and left the entrepreneur no better off than he was before he borrowed. A rising equity market allowed entrepre-neurs to extract value from a company, so debt fell out of favor as a financ-ing mechanism. But curiously, while interest rates were falling, a new group of bond investors was emerging who noticed some curious things about the bond market.

Enter the carry trade, in which investors borrow long and invest short. It doesn't matter who first noticed that short-term interest rates were dropping more rapidly than long-term rates, but whoever it was could im-mediately make money on the spread between the two. In the mid-1990s, it was possible to borrow money in Japan at essentially zero interest and invest it in 10-year U.S. Treasuries, which were paying a risk-free return in excess of 6 percent, or in higher-risk junk bonds that were paying in excess of 12 percent. That was the best kind of investing possible: there was little or no risk, and money could be rolled over and reinvested every quarter, compounding the return. This ability to make money off of the differential between short and long rates has made money for investors until quite recently, when short-term U.S. Treasury rates and long-term rates finally began to converge. It is still possible to make money on the carry trade, but now you have to look abroad, put together combinations of short-term notes from one country and long-term bonds from another. The risks are higher, but with the improvement of global economic con-ditions outside the United States, many of these long-term credits now carry investment-grade ratings, meaning that their perceived risks are about the same as high-grade U.S. corporate bonds.

Is it still possible to make money in bonds in a rising-interest-rate environment? You can when the interest rate yield curve inverts. The interest rate yield curve is really nothing more than a comparative indicator of interest rates over time. The curve begins at the short end, that is, 3-month or 1-year bonds, and finishes at the long end, where maturities are anywhere from 10 to 30 years, depending upon the issuing authority. Most central banks spend their time attempting to control the economy in the present tense, so they only worry about short-term interest rates. They allow the markets to worry about future expectations about the economy, and so allow the markets to set long-term interest rates.

Normally, when central banks drive up short rates, it is to bring inflation under control, since high inflation is a major threat to economic growth. Inflation raises the prices of goods and squeezes profits, which limits how much of the prices paid for raw materials can be passed on to consumers. Rising inflation has the power to slow an economy down, which puts workers into the unemployment line and exacerbates social tensions—and can ultimately drive politicians from office. While central bankers recognize that the economy needs a bit of inflation as a stimulus for growth, no one likes high inflation, which is typically perceived as anything above 2.5 percent annually. At that rate, prices will double only once in a generation, allowing consumer incomes and productivity to keep up with rising prices. Raising interest rates makes consumers think twice about buying goods in the present that they are going to have to pay off in the future, in the form of mortgages and credit card interest payments on unpaid balances.

As a central bank begins to raise short-term rates, three things can happen to the yield curve. The long end can rise along with the short end, indicating that investors believe it will take many more interest rate hikes to bring inflation into line. This scenario is generally a sign of a strong economy that could overheat, but it often accompanies a rising stock market. Second, the curve can begin to flatten, indicating that investors believe that the economy will come into balance at some point. Finally, the curve can invert, and long interest rates can be lower than short rates. When this happens, investors are betting that economic activity will slow significantly. In fact, over the past thirty years or so, inverted yield curves have been fairly accurate predictors of coming recessions, especially if they persist for any length of time and if the spread widens past about half a percentage point.

So what do you do with that knowledge? The interest rate environment is often a good barometer for what you should do with your money. In the 1970s, when interest rates were rising sharply, you were punished if you did anything else with your money but invest it in cash. Do you remember that period? You could purchase zero coupon bonds that paid 16 percent, but stocks were doing nothing. In the 1980s, as rates began to drop, you were penalized for holding cash, and made out if you were in the stock market early. As the bond market has globalized, during the 1990s and early 2000s, it was good to invest both in stocks and in the carry trade. Today, as rates are rising again around the world, investors are defensively fleeing back into cash or investing in high-quality stocks on the expectation that once interest rates begin to fall again, these investments will provide double growth, in the form of price appreciation and higher dividends. It is a sensible strategy, but it is one that punishes strong companies that do not pay a dividend. Many of the high-technology companies fit that description. They have neither markets growing rapidly enough to justify their high multiples (as they did in the past) nor dividends to entice buyers.

Finally, the choice between investing during a rising-interest-rate environment and during a falling-interest-rate period has a lot to do with risk tolerance. A rising-rate environment is a time for businesses to search out and invest in productivity tools, the software and machinery that companies need to keep their costs from rising and their profits from falling. Companies that improve logistical flow, throughput, the speed of transactions, and hourly output per worker are all good choices, and these are not always the companies you think they are. For example, in our current energy environment, the price of energy is partially the cost of extracting it, but also partially the cost of bringing it to market—in the case of natural gas, pipelines and special pressurized ships that transport it. For coal, there is a serious shortage of railcars and rail lines that can carry low-sulfur coal from the mines of the northwestern United States to the power plants of the northeast and central states. And for many commodities, there are now not enough river barges—to carry wheat and corn and soybeans, not to mention coal and oil. River barges might be slow, but they are so much cheaper than any other form of transportation that they can more than overcome their lack of speed in the form of lower prices. That makes them a productivity tool. The same thing goes for cranes at docks that unload giant container cargo ships and the equipment that gets those containers and other loads onto trucks quickly and safely. When most people think of productivity nowadays, they think of software, but all sorts of hardware solutions provide a good investment. What do all of these productivity tools have in common? They are all engineered products, so investing in engineering firms is also a good bet.

Business reorganization is another form of productivity tool that does well in a rising-interest-rate environment, particularly consulting services and large business process civil engineering firms. Most companies have been reluctant to spend cash over the past five years, preferring to keep it as a hedge against future inflation, which has resulted in a capital spending drought. But companies know that money spent on productivity improvements at the right time can pay off. That is what's happening in Japan right now. After years of zero inflation and zero interest rates, Japanese companies are beginning to spend on the next generation of industrial machinery to ensure that they do not get passed by China as Asia's leading industrial power. That spending has paid off in a 50 percent rise in Japan's Nikkei index over the past two years.

Let's review. When interest rates are falling, that is generally a good time to invest in most stocks. When they are rising, that is generally a good time to focus on productivity investments. When interest rates are falling, it makes sense to take advantage of the different speeds at which rates fall by playing the carry trade, but when interest rates rise, it is a good time to unwind your trades and sit on the sidelines in cash, collecting a nice interest rate and waiting for the next opportunity to emerge. As with most investments, interest rate environments are not an absolute signal but another set of metrics that you should observe. Rates can help to guide you in your investment decisions. Finally, remember again to always be looking beyond your borders, for while the carry trade might be dying with one set of bonds, it might be alive and well with another.

CHAPTER 12

ALPHA *versus* BETA

Alpha is a technical term that refers to the difference between a stock or a mutual fund's expected performance and its actual performance. If the market expects your fund to rise by 20 percent this year and the fund manager produces a 25 percent gain, the extra five points is alpha, and that extra five percentage points determines the size of his bonus. The biggest rule in becoming a winning investor is always to look for situations that produce alpha. Alpha is opportunity. Alpha is what makes you better than the next guy, and ultimately it is alpha that will make you richer.

You need to care about alpha because Wall Street cares about it. Wall Street doesn't measure money managers and corporate CEOs on how well they performed in the past. The past evaporates the moment it happens. Wall Street bets on future expectations, and if you have performed well in the past, look out, because Wall Street's expectations about your future performance will rise. Think of it this way: For three years in a row, you buy your wife flowers for her birthday. The next year, you buy her a nice piece of jewelry. If you go back to flowers the following year, you're going to get the cold stare, a distant thank-you, and her cold shoulder in bed. If you buy her a piece of jewelry that is just as nice as the one you bought her the year before, you're going to get a polite thank-you and maybe a peck on the cheek, but not much more. You have raised the bar on your wife's expectations, and now anything you do that does not meet her *neue Weltanschauung*—her new view of the world, which dictates how she acts—will generate disappointment. It's human nature, and it works on Wall Street the same way it works in relationships.

As a result, most professional fund managers work to dampen your enthusiasm about their performance. All those mutual fund marketing prospectuses say, "Past performance is no indication of future results," and that's designed to keep you from getting your hopes up. All those CEOs who "manage" their earnings to meet Wall Street's expectations are doing it to keep their stock from crashing in a tidal wave of disappointment. These expectations help explain the wave of corporate fraud a couple of years ago. Wall Street's performance demands had gotten so out of line that some corporate chieftains could only make their numbers by faking them. (I'm not blaming Wall Street for the fraud. Managers, after all, did have the choice of sucking it up and taking a hit to their stock price—and to their bonuses.)

At a certain point in their careers, nearly all fund managers and CEOs wind up managing expectations instead of working harder to produce good results. So when you see a top-ranked manager suddenly have a mediocre year, don't hold on to your mutual fund shares expecting that he or she will have a rebound. Go someplace else. Once that alpha is gone, it's time to find another waterfall.

For a very long time, since the end of World War II, in fact, you could find alpha by spreading risk. I have already mentioned the two models for investing. One is a process of spreading risk called asset allocation. The idea behind asset allocation is that you are willing to sacrifice a small amount of gain in order to shed a larger amount of risk. You get a lot of small buckets instead of one large one and then find waterfalls in the form of fund managers who are doing well and place your buckets under them. If you find half a dozen good money managers and put some money with each of them, when one of them has a bad year, it will be offset by someone else who is having a great year. Even if you were to choose half a dozen truly mediocre money managers, the range of performances would still beat the market by a small percentage year after year.

Asset allocation worked well for a long time because of the Wall Street adage that "a rising tide lifts all boats." The period after World War II was one of prolonged prosperity, so that long-only investment strategies worked. During this time almost any investment style worked. During the 1980s, the *Wall Street Journal* proved that you could outperform the market just by throwing darts at the stock pages. You could spread your risk randomly and be sure that something would work in your favor.

Surprisingly, the top investors ignore alpha. They look at something called *beta,* which measures an investment's risk. How risky is the type of business, and what is the amount of risk in the financial structure or leverage of a company? Beta measures the risk of the company relative to the risk of the stock market in general. With greater risk, as measured by larger variability in profits (business or operating risk), the company should have a larger beta. And with greater leverage (a higher debt-to-value ratio) and increasing financial risk, the company's stock should also have a larger beta. With a larger beta, an investor should expect the possibility of a greater return on his investment. Generally, the higher the beta, the greater the chance that your return will be superior in an up market, but in a down market, there is a greater likelihood that your stock will underperform.

When Warren Buffett invests, for example, he begins with companies that are underpriced according to Benjamin Graham's formula. While the beta of an average-risk firm in the stock market is 1.00, Buffett's companies are often high-beta stocks, because there is some perceived risk in either the company's operations or its financial structure that is pulling down the stock price. Once that perception is corrected, the beta will drop, but the price of the stock will rise, much in the same manner that bond prices rise as their yields fall, and vice versa. Buffett looks for stocks that rise as they become safer investments, as measured by the capital asset pricing model (CAPM), which is used by many market analysts in their valuation process. CAPM says that the expected return of any security you buy should equal whatever a risk-free security should cost plus the risk premium for owning something that is not risk-free. The commonly used formula for calculating CAPM is as follows:

Expected Return = Risk-Free Rate + (Market Return − Risk-Free Rate)
× Beta

Let's say that the risk-free rate is the 5.25 percent return on 3-month Treasury notes and that the S&P 500 is expected to average an 11 percent return next year. You want to buy a stock whose beta is 1.5. (You can find the current beta by going to the library and looking it up in *Value Line,* or by using one of the myriad of stock services found on the Internet.) The CAPM for the stock you are thinking about buying is 5.25% + (11% − 5.25%) × 1.5, or 13.875%. This means that the stock you are considering purchasing must yield a return of nearly 14 percent in order for it to be worth putting in your portfolio as opposed to something else.

Look at it this way: in general—not always, but in general—the stock market is an accurate reflection of the economy. When the economy is healthy, you will make the most money by finding the stocks that will outperform the market at large. These are often higher-beta stocks. You still need to do the basic research to find out why the stock has the potential to be an outperformer before you make an investment, but if you use betas as a screen to narrow your universe, you will be somewhat ahead of the game when you begin drilling down. In down or falling markets, investors become more risk-averse, and they punish companies that have high beta by disinvesting, so the price falls. Once a stock falls from investor grace, it can take a long time for it to return to favor, so as a rule, high-beta stocks that fall out of favor are not going to come back soon when investors return to the stock markets. The quick victors will be lower-beta stocks, which may not have fallen as far or might even have risen during a down market.

What about markets that seem to lack direction? Neither alpha nor beta is much help, because when the market is in the doldrums, it is harder for managers to find alpha without taking on more risk, and it is difficult to make a case for beta investing, because then you wind up in a buy-and-hold situation as you wait for a trend to emerge. I believe that hedge funds did well over the past five years because fund managers could find informational black holes to exploit, not because they were masters of terrific alpha strategies. As time goes on and more hedge funds are created, the probability that a manager can produce significant amounts of alpha diminishes. In August 2006, Bill Gross, the great bond manager at PIMCO, complained publicly that it was becoming increasingly difficult for him to create alpha, to beat the market consistently. If he can't do so, that's yet another push toward cash or other alternative investments, such as real estate, art, or antique furniture. I still prefer alpha to beta, because I prefer looking for opportunity in all sorts of places—allowing my imagination to move about freely—to the rigors of sifting through the market for situations that might have a small potential for gain.

CHAPTER 13

CARTELS *versus* OPEN COMPETITION

Economists can drive investors crazy because they have an exception for every rule. Any good economist will tell you that monopolies and cartels are ultimately bad. They impede competition and economic efficiency and add costs to an economic system. Many of these same economists will then tell you with a straight face that sometimes a monopoly is good, such as in electric power generation, because competition, which empowers many small companies, impedes the large capital investments needed to establish and maintain a national power grid, for example. Then they will twist themselves into pretzels when it comes to so-called natural monopolies, such as Microsoft, which for nearly thirty years has generated huge returns for its investors, even as it became an increasingly fierce competitor in operating-system software.

So which is the better investment? Is it the company with a lock on its market, which can determine both the pace and depth of change, or is it the company in open competition, where a winner today may become tomorrow's loser? For the ordinary investor, the answer isn't easy. Competition looks like the way to go, because the shares of hot new companies shoot upward like rockets to the moon. But more often than not they crash, wiping out shareholder capital and leaving lawsuits and recrimination in their wake.

So which way do you go? Large institutions have a large-cap and big-company bias because their ownership rules force that bias on them. Institutional share owners have diversification rules that prohibit them from owning more than a couple of percentage points of the shares of any given company. If you squander that on allocations of small-cap shares, you will have to own many more companies than if you own large-cap shares. And one of the things you don't want to do as an institutional investor is own too many volatile high-beta shares in companies that might fail. As an institutional owner, you don't mind allocating some of the money you might put into small-caps into venture capital instead, because the returns are greater, but in the long run, building a portfolio with somewhere between twenty-five and fifty large-cap names is the easiest, most defensible, and safest way to go.

But you are not an institution. Just as you should not attempt to emulate most investment professionals, you should not try to run your own portfolio like an institution. When markets are in a downturn or just coming off of one, large-cap stocks can be a good protective investment, because their long track record of paying dividends and economies of scale allows them to keep their profits rolling in even as the economy slows. Individually, large-caps can and do suffer losses. Companies in certain sectors, such as autos, housing, computers, pharmaceuticals, banks, and insurance, often lose money in economic downturns, either because what they sell is sensitive to interest rates or because they have inventory hangovers of overpriced goods from better times. Many companies try to maintain lean inventories to prevent such losses, but it's a persistent danger despite the best efforts of corporate managers. Indeed, there is nothing sacred about large companies. It's just that relative to small companies, they stumble less often, and when they do fail, they have more resources to tide them over until they resolve their problems. Large U.S. companies currently have more than $1 trillion in cash on hand, and even the worst has many more weapons at its disposal for making a comeback than any smaller company.

So do you stay with large-caps that can create monopoly conditions and forsake the opportunities that can come from investing in smaller, more rapidly growing companies? It depends upon what kinds of returns you want, how much time you have for homework, and how well you can use knowledge to minimize your risks. Remember the CAPM formula from the last chapter? You can use it as a screening tool to improve your returns and to give you a set of indicators about how well you can do without taking on undue risk. For example, let's say the risk-free return is 5.25

percent. A CAPM of 10.5 percent would give you a 100 percent boost over the risk-free return. But how do you find that? Look for stocks whose CAPM is somewhere between 15 and 20, and find the best ones in that group. If they do only half as well as they need to do to reach the higher level of return, you can sell and still have done much better than the risk-free return. In fact, in a down market, it is likely you will have outperformed the market as a whole. You don't need to get the whole return, just enough to satisfy your own goals.

As I noted earlier, the markets provide opportunities for you to lay off a lot of your risk while giving you the opportunity to keep much of your gain. You ought to build your portfolio around that concept. One way to approach this problem is to look not at the stocks you might purchase, but rather the markets they serve. If you learn to shift your vision this way, all sorts of opportunities will emerge, because suddenly, what was big can become small, and vice versa. Look at a company like Starbucks. It is the giant of its field, with thousands of shops serving a wide variety of coffee-based drinks in the United States and Europe every day. By one standard, Starbucks is a huge company. In 2007 it had annual revenues of nearly $9.4 billion. But if you look at Starbucks in a different light, it is really just an up-and-coming smaller company. After all, it has barely penetrated markets outside the United States and Europe—particularly Asia—and it could conceivably continue to grow at a strong pace for several years to come. In that respect, Starbucks has more in common with small, up-and-coming growth companies than the much larger companies before it on the Fortune 500 list.

What you are looking for, then, is growth potential of a company within its industry or, even better, its ability to find new markets or new products to expand beyond the industry or geographical region it already serves. Google is a great example of a company that is a giant in the developed world but still has room to grow as emerging markets increase their Internet usage.

Still, this chapter is about cartels, not growth stocks. It turns out that even cartels don't really like cartels. When the oil ministers of OPEC meet in Vienna to decide how much oil to pump, they might control production, but they don't really make much effort to monitor who is cheating.

When OPEC first came to prominence during the 1970s, the oil ministers thought that they could control price by controlling the supply—how much they pumped—but they quickly discovered that their members would cheat the cartel by pumping more, because local considerations very quickly trumped the discipline of the cartel. One country wanted more money for education, another for weapons, and still another to provide allowances for a huge royal family. It didn't matter: OPEC would pass pumping resolutions, and its members would violate them. Without control of its members, OPEC quickly discovered that its own rigidity about supply was just an incentive for the energy companies to look for oil elsewhere.

The same holds true for diamonds. Once upon a time, South Africa's great De Beers firm controlled the diamond industry, forcing smaller producers to sell stones at De Beers's determined wholesale prices to the Central Selling Organization. The CSO then forced jewelers to take whatever stones they were sold, so jewelers had to find ways to dispose of unwanted stones. The trade in these low-quality stones spawned an international industry, lowering the cost of diamonds, an unintended consequence. Meanwhile, in the late 1980s and early 1990s, diamond-rich Russia, in need of money, began to sell stones to the same jewelers who were purchasing from the CSO. Then Canada and Australia discovered diamonds, and the CSO monopoly was broken. De Beers was forced to reinvent itself as a marketing organization; the CSO still exists, but it is no longer the all-powerful monopoly it once was.

Cartels? Pretty useless, but good to watch, because they will always spawn new businesses attempting to beat them. That's where the real investment opportunities are.

CHAPTER 14

PROTECTIONISM *versus* FOCUS ON THE FUTURE

The classic company story about protectionism is that of Xerox, which began its life when the Haloid Company bought a patent for dry copying—that's what xerography means—in 1942. Over the next thirty years or so, the company built up a wall of patents that made it feel secure from competition, even though other companies had developed copiers that used variations of Xerox's technology. Xerox didn't seem to care, as they "owned" more than 70 percent of the worldwide copier market. And then one day, it all fell apart.

Fuji, a Japanese licensee of Xerox, discovered a maxim that has made technology one of the least protectable attributes of a company's strength: "What one person can create, another can learn." Fuji didn't copy Xerox's technology; it merely reasoned that if it was possible to do xerography one way, another way was probably available. Fuji figured it out, adding superior optics and manufacturing capabilities to machines that began to beat the pants off of Xerox's, first in overseas markets and then, finally, in the United States. Xerox still competes in the document business, but technology has changed so much that it no longer dominates. With its diminished lead has gone its stock price and status as one of the greatest technology companies of the past fifty years.

Technology isn't a wall of protection for companies. Often, entire industries will use tariffs and trade barriers to keep out competitors, reasoning that they have a "natural" right to the markets they have built up and developed. But capitalism is a cruel master, and there is no such thing as a "right" or "entitlement" to a market. Companies retain markets by staying smarter and working harder than their competitors—period. But try telling that to most chief executives. They will ramble on about all the steps they have taken to remain competitive and then rush to testify before Congress about how much protection they need from foreign companies threatening to take their markets away. When most successful companies talk about competition, what they really mean is the competition they can easily dominate. Intel and Advanced Micro Devices have been locked in competition in the microprocessor market for years, and the two companies own the sector. But should a third company come in, say, a Chinese microprocessor firm, the two will unite to scream "unfair competition." Early in 2006, the Chinese attempted to introduce their own standard for cell phones. The companies in that market, normally intense rivals, suddenly united and threatened to cut off China's access to technology. The Chinese backed off, but it left a bitter taste, and it is obvious that China will soon come back to the marketplace with a new technology, eager to conquer the market by creating a dominant new technology.

Protectionism comes in many forms, and no matter how much lip service companies pay to the idea of competition, most companies will take all the protection they can get. What they really want to be is monopolists! But are monopolies good investments? For years, Microsoft was. It owned the operating system market and, by extension, the business software market and, through that, lots of smaller markets as well. Microsoft earned billions of dollars in profits, enriched its stockholders and employees, and turned Bill Gates into the richest man on the planet. But nobody likes monopolists, even when, as Gates would point out, the monopoly was the natural outcome of the company's work. When both the U.S. government and the European Union began to call Microsoft's monopoly into question, the company claimed that all it was doing was making better-integrated software than its competitors. To give competitors access to its code was tantamount to giving away its technological edge. Unfortunately for Microsoft, neither the U.S. government nor the EU bought that claim, and Microsoft had to "unbundle" its software and allow competitors to sell products that would work on the Microsoft operating system. Since then, the company has lost some of its competitive fire, and while Microsoft will continue to grow at a substantial rate, many analysts argue that Microsoft is now a mature company with its best years behind it. Perhaps. Perhaps not.

The opposite of monopoly, for an investor's purpose, is companies focused on the future. It doesn't have to be a company. Look at Harvard versus, say, Penn State. Harvard has only one campus, and its faculty has resisted exporting the Harvard experience. Penn State has dozens of campuses around Pennsylvania and is willing to export its education services wherever there is demand. In China and India, where there is an enormous demand for education, certainly most of the best students would prefer to come to the United States and attend Harvard. But if another U.S. institution decided to set up satellite campuses in China and India and provide them with teachers, staff, and libraries of a quality equal to that provided in the States, do you think those satellite campuses would go empty? They would be bursting at the seams within a few years. Moreover, the university making that investment would also profit from the land it owns surrounding the campus, which can be turned into dorms and apartments that can be rented out or industrial parks that profit from the university's research and pay fees to the university, along the Stanford/ Palo Alto model.

Companies have an obligation to shareholders to remain firmly focused on the future. After all, stock markets judge them not on the basis of what they did last month or last quarter but on what they are likely to do next month and next quarter. The markets may use current data to make an estimate, but don't ever forget that Wall Street is nearly always about the future. When a company does not meet analysts' estimates and its stock is downgraded, it is because the company failed to meet future expectations. This scrutiny places many companies and CEOs in an awkward position. In a tightly competitive market, an analyst's "sell" rating can cripple a company's future ability to raise capital, forcing it from the equity markets into the bond market or into bank borrowing, often at a higher interest rate than it wants to pay. Think of bank credit ratings and loan sharks. If the bank turns you down for a loan because you have a bad credit rating—or, put another way, because you did not live up to banks' and credit card companies' expectations about how you would handle your finances in the future—you must borrow from sources, such as finance companies, that charge higher interest rates. And if you have really bad credit, you might be forced to borrow from a loan shark.

It's the same with companies. Once one has been downgraded, it has only a small window in which to get its house in order, a couple of quarters at the most. If it fails, Wall Street loses interest entirely, the CEO is often forced out, and the company becomes a candidate for takeover or reorganization.

During the years 2000 to 2003, a series of scandals erupted at large companies around the United States and, eventually, around the world. We describe them collectively as accounting scandals, because they all involved cooking the books in some way, either by creating paper profits where none existed or by shifting sales from one quarter to another. All of this was done in the name of "managing earnings." Enron, Ahold, Parmalat, Adelphia Cable, and more than a dozen other companies propped up their earnings or sales to keep Wall Street's analyst community happy so that they could either continue to raise money in the equity markets through new share sales or borrow in the bond markets at preferential rates. Enron was the worst example, creating a wholly fictitious trading operation and numerous side companies into which it could dump its accumulating debts, just so that its profits would continue to astound Wall Street and attract investors. This kind of behavior is not a focus on the future but rather a surrender to the past, a panicked realization that there is no magic bullet or special formula for making money. As Michael Armstrong, the CEO of AT&T, said of his competitor WorldCom after its fake accounting was revealed, "We knew their numbers were too good to be true, but we thought that our numbers were a reflection of our failure, not that they were cheating. Think of all the companies that went out of business that assumed that [their results] were real." Armstrong couldn't know this until after the fact, though, and his efforts to bring AT&T up to WorldCom's (false) standard of performance wound up damaging the company, which was saved only by a merger with Southwestern Bell.

When a company or an industry or even a nation begins to cry protectionism, it is nearly always a sign to move on. There is no waterfall to be found in companies that depend on their ability to keep competitors at bay. Another company is almost always bound to come up with a way around any barriers a company might create. Even if those boundaries seem permanent, they never last.

PART IV

CHANGING OPPORTUNITIES

Several years ago, I went on a photo safari in Africa, and the guide who took us out onto the veldt told us that one of the best ways to get good pictures was to get up on the little rock-and-dirt outcroppings that dot the plains. From there, he said, we would have a better vantage point, and we would see things we never saw before. He also told us to spend some time just staring—not taking photos, just allowing our vision to expand. I didn't know exactly what he meant, but I did as he recommended, and a funny thing began to happen. After an hour or so, and then in coming days, not only did my eyes readjust their focus, but so did the rest of my senses. I could begin to see individual blades of grass and leaves at much greater distances, and I could hear animal sounds and smell the many varieties of plant and animal life out on the veldt. As a result, I was able to take much better pictures.

I know that has a bit of a New Age, touchy-feely sound to it, but some of the smartest investors I know are smart precisely because they have trained themselves to see what others cannot. Their insights become the strongest-performing investments of tomorrow. I often tell clients that one of the most important components of outperformance is the ability to see what others will also see, but before they do. Remember Colonel Boyd and the OODA loop? As the loop is meant to get you from observation to action, it is most valuable when it helps you reduce the time between each action. If you think of a clock metaphor, most investors—even most institutional investors—get into an investment somewhere between 10 P.M. and midnight. Think how much better you could do if you could observe an opportunity at 9 A.M.

and get in by noon. You would be in a position to sell to all the other folks rushing in much later, pocket your profits, and move on to the next opportunity. Best of all, you would almost always be on the right side of the trade.

How early is too early? I think that the general rule is, if you get a hunch that no one else has, it might be too early. The best way to test your hunches is to formulate them into stories. Let's say it is the middle of 2004 and you are down in Mexico reading the papers, and you see that there is a growing feud between the president, Vicente Fox, and the leftist mayor of Mexico City, Andrés Manuel López Obrador, also known as AMLO. You type "AMLO" into Google, and you find out that he is thinking of running for president when Fox's term is up at the end of 2006 but that he is not given much chance. You might file this away and, from time to time, check up on AMLO by having Google alert you every time a reference to AMLO or Vicente Fox appears in a certain context. Within a year, you have a bulging file of notes, and you notice that the relationship between the two men has deteriorated to the point where there is talk of impeaching AMLO. When you first noticed AMLO in the newspaper, you were at one minute past midnight into a new day, but a year later, you are probably at 6 A.M. Nothing is happening. The Mexican economy is rolling along, and you begin to widen your search by typing "Mexican economy" into Google. You begin to see reports about Mexican credit card growth, how great the Mexican mortgage industry has become, and how many people are buying houses. You also begin to notice that in Chiapas state, there is growing unrest, and that in Oaxaca, civil servants, especially teachers, are complaining about the lack of funding.

What you now have are a couple of dots, certainly not enough to form a pattern. But by the spring of 2006, a pattern begins to coalesce. AMLO has decided to run for president; Fox's party, the PAN, is in disarray; and the traditional holder of power, the PRI, is wracked with infighting. Political pundits are still arguing that AMLO has no chance, but the Mexican peso begins to wobble, and the stock market begins to flatten from its torrid growth of a year before. Part of that wobble is due to the worldwide correction among emerging markets in May and June 2006, but some of it is based on local news and evidence. It is now 10 A.M. on the uncertainty clock.

If you are an investor with an appetite for risk, June would probably have been a good time to invest in peso futures or to begin scrutinizing the Bolsa, the Mexican stock market, for opportunities, either to short or to buy. If AMLO comes to power, who is hurt and who benefits? What of the currency, or Mexico's bonds? All of these questions begin to become clearer. Now the political pundits are beginning to be joined by the economic analysts. A consensus is beginning to form. In June the majority of analysts insist that the upcoming election will go smoothly, but there is a small minority who argue that it will not. You decide to go with the latter group, as there is more upside for you in the downside of Mexican politics. Meanwhile, the conventional wisdom still holds that Felipe Calderón, Fox's candidate to succeed him, will win and that the transition will be smooth. No one reckons that AMLO might throw a monkey wrench into the works.

But he does. The election takes place, and AMLO loses—by a hairsbreadth. His followers camp out in the Zócalo, Mexico City's huge main square, and his party's politicians begin to disrupt Mexico's Congress. All through the summer, the disputed vote count paralyzes Mexico, and suddenly, the peso wobbles a bit more, as does the Bolsa. Conventional wisdom still calls for a smooth transition, but increasingly, it looks as if AMLO or his supporters might touch off an uprising. By September, when Mexico's electoral tribunal certifies Calderón as the winner, the damage has been done. Though there is no revolt, Mexico's economy will now likely be hampered for the next six years, as Calderón, who is an adroit leader, is nonetheless hampered by a need to keep the left at bay. You emerge as the winner just as the pundits are figuring out that it is time to backtrack on the Bolsa.

That, of course, is just a hypothetical example of how one can learn to read the landscape. An easier one might be the following scenario: You take a trip to Asia, maybe on business, perhaps for pleasure, and you see that the economies of Singapore and Thailand and half a dozen other places, including China, are booming. People have cars; everyone has a cell phone. Clearly, prosperity has returned to Asia. How do you invest in it? Do you buy the shares of luxury-goods companies, or perhaps the large global packaged-goods companies, such as Colgate-Palmolive, Procter & Gamble, and Unilever? Well, you ask, what do hardworking Asians want the most? The answer, not surprisingly, is the same things you do. They want more leisure time with which to enjoy their newfound wealth, and they want to travel to new places, just like you. Of course, they also have no social security provisions, so they need a mechanism by which they can save for retirement, perhaps life insurance or an annuity, and they are intent on educating their children, so perhaps you want to also look at the for-profit schools springing up all over Asia. Or perhaps you want to invest in the people themselves, in their own new start-ups and businesses that have potential. Those are all 10 A.M. investments. While Asians will purchase more packaged goods, you have to ask yourself, how long will it take for Asian demand to have a measurable impact on the bottom line of a western company whose profits are measured in billions of dollars?

If you are going to spot new opportunities, you have to learn how to take the conventional wisdom and question it and then ask yourself lots of what-if questions. Not notional what-ifs, such as what if there is another terror attack, but realistic what-ifs, such as what if Africa becomes more stable? A quick look at Africa will show you that some of the most active and booming stock markets are there, but they are small and hard to invest in. Nevertheless, you might think about what happens as Africa puts its problems behind it. Those are questions worth asking. So too are questions about Latin America. After a dozen years in which Latin America seemed to be on a path to reform, growth appears to have stalled in some nations, including Brazil. Nevertheless, stock markets are moving ahead strongly in Argentina, which was an economic basket case only three years ago, and, shockingly, in Venezuela, which has leftist Hugo Chavez in charge. Read the press, and the middle class is howling. Look at the Caracas stock market, and it is saying something else entirely. (It turns out that although the middle class doesn't much like Chavez, currency controls keep Venezuelans from investing abroad, so they put their money into the stock market, a bet on the day when Chavez might leave.) When you can figure out what the differences mean, you will be able to determine whether you have an investment possibility or a trap to avoid.

CHAPTER 15

ENTITLEMENT *versus* OPPORTUNITY

Entitlements are things to which you believe you have a right; opportunities are things for which you are willing to take a risk. In the United States and much of the rest of the world, pensions, social security, medical benefits, and the like are entitlements. Workers "earned" them by their willingness to engage in labor stoppages and slowdowns, and those entitlements, due to their huge size, now threaten to bring down many large companies and even governments. In most of the world, where populations are younger and governments are poorer, there are few entitlements, except in China and India, where there are small elite groups, such as the Communist Party in China or the upper castes in India, who are "entitled" to skim off the top of society. In many other nations where the base of wealth is small, oligarchies of intermarried families control much of the wealth. In Brazil, for example, twenty thousand families control 80 percent of the wealth.

Americans are used to investing in the forces of opportunity—after all, that was what the Internet and telecom booms were all about—and we tend to shun investing in the forces of entitlement. But should we? A look back at the three best-performing stock markets over the past five years shows that all three were in nations controlled by small oligarchies—Mexico, Saudi Arabia, and Kuwait. In Kuwait, the ruling Al-Sabah family controls or has a stake in every business worth owning, and in Saudi Arabia, the princely families related to the Sauds own most of the wealth. While Mexico continues to modernize in fits and starts, for years financial success has depended upon the political patronage of the PRI, until recently the major political party in Mexico.

This anecdotal evidence does not mean that you should invest in nations ruled by oligarchies. Rather, it means that you should invest where there are savvy investors. In capital-scarce nations tightly controlled by small groups, money is not usually handed out to idiot relatives. This isn't a hard-and-fast rule: in Indonesia, where corruption was rampant under the control of General Suharto, far too much money was siphoned off into enterprises controlled by his family members. Those companies were not opportunities in Suharto's days. But now, as a reform government has taken control, the companies are gradually being sold off, representing good prospects for the future.

Often, the question with entitlement-driven states is one of degree. Under Boris Yeltsin, Russia was a freer society than it is under Vladimir Putin. But under Yeltsin, Russia's economy was run by a tight band of oligarchs who frequently used gangster tactics to force smaller competitors out of business. Putin has pushed out most of the oligarchs and has consolidated control of Russia's largest industry, energy, under a single company, Gazprom. Gazprom uses tactics not that different from the oligarchs to muscle its way into the investments in and around Russia. But because there is so much money to be made in Russian energy, many investors are willing to overlook Gazprom's business tactics for the opportunity to invest in what will probably be a winning company for many years to come. That confidence, in turn, has helped to lift other stocks on the Russian stock market, as investors can see the benefits of Putin's carefully controlled economy trickling down to ordinary Russians. Salaries have increased dramatically, and spending on everything from cars and cell phones to real estate and travel has gone through the roof. Russia is on its way to becoming a middle-class country, and rising middle-class countries make good investments.

Sometimes even the mere promise of reform can set a stock market on fire. Egypt has been the third-best performing stock market in the Middle East over the past several years, largely on the promise of free elections, legal reforms, and the probable retirement of longtime president Hosni Mubarak. Even though Mubarak's retirement might open the door to an Islamist government, many investors are betting that Egypt's 78 million people, a predominantly young population, will prefer opportunity to radical religious politics. As Egypt's industries expand and generate more jobs, the nation will become a more promising venue for further investment. Moreover, there are now millions of Egyptians living abroad, and they are beginning to send money home, to build better homes for themselves and to invest in small businesses run by family members. That's another investment opportunity, and wherever you see locals investing in the future, you ought to be looking in that direction as well.

While I much prefer to invest in opportunity, that does not mean that there isn't money to be made by investing in entitlement. Indeed, as the cost of entitlements rises and individuals refuse to give them up, some strong bond investments emerge. Nations with strong social security systems, such as the United States and France, are going to have to keep interest rates high in order to lure the capital needed to fund their systems without raising taxes. But there is a downside: the need for entitlement funding can lead, as it did in the 1970s and the early 1980s, to interest rate hikes so high that they begin to crowd out other types of investment. As I write, a large wall of liquidity, surplus cash, and profits has kept such a process from happening. Interest rates are still reasonable, but we are probably on the cusp of high government rates having a negative impact on other forms of investment. That is why, as of this writing, new Fed chairman Ben Bernanke has been so cautious about raising interest rates despite signs that inflation may be rising. He will be challenged to keep rates from slowing growth so dramatically that he drags the U.S. economy into a recession. This problem will persist for at least several years, or until politicians figure out how to reform Social Security without tearing it apart.

Another way to profit from entitlement is to take a look at the increasing number of state-run oil companies, such as Petróleos de Venezuela; PEMEX, the Mexican oil company; or Gazprom. Since the run-up of oil prices began three years ago, many nations have decided that oil and natural gas are part of the "patrimony of the state" and that a larger share of their profits ought to go into the public coffers rather than into oil company pockets. Don't fret for the oil companies. Their profits are still enormous. But the state oil monopolies now developing are in effect entitlement centers and thus are guaranteed to be inefficient. Nevertheless, they have enormous amounts of money to invest, and many of them will never develop sufficient expertise to run an efficient oil industry. What they refuse to pay their oil company partners in lifting fees, they will more than make up in the fees paid to energy service companies at all stages, from exploration to refining.

There are still other ways that entitlement generates opportunity, and vice versa. In many nations, there are long-established bureaucracies that wield tremendous power. As these governments seek solutions in the private sector, even for the purpose of protecting their own power, they nevertheless generate opportunities for small companies to devise mechanisms to improve bureaucratic efficiency. In the United States, dozens of companies in and around Washington, D.C., such as SAIC, Halliburton, and others, have cashed in on the steady shift of government responsibilities from the public to the private sector. It isn't that the bureaucracies and their entitlements have been destroyed—far from it. Today, the path of contracts and handouts is dominated by fewer firms with better profit margins.

Still another way to profit from the entitlement/opportunity binary is to follow the law. Legislation that empowers one group by providing it with funding is an entitlement for that group—but an opportunity for investors. Whenever you look at a piece of legislation with funding attached, ask yourself who will be hurt and who will be helped. If it is a huge transportation or infrastructure bill of the type that comes along once every decade or so, does that become a signal to invest in the civil engineering and construction cycle? If a bill goes through Congress that changes the depreciation schedule for businesses, what is added and what is taken away? And remember, whatever you see in the United States today will be replicated tomorrow in more than a hundred other nations, some large and some small. In those countries too, opportunity is being born out of entitlements, and vice versa. You just have to learn how to see the one in the other, and both in each, and then invest accordingly.

CHAPTER 16

FAD *versus* TREND

Things are seldom what they seem,
  Skim milk masquerades as cream;
Highlows pass as patent leathers;
  Jackdaws strut in peacock's feathers.

So sings Buttercup in Gilbert and Sullivan's *HMS Pinafore*. The line, first performed in 1878, is as true today as it was then. We are easily fooled by the appearance of truth, because we all want to be believers. Nowhere is this truer than in investing. Everyone wants to believe that the stock or bond or portfolio they have assembled is going to be the one that turns into a fortune.

As an individual investor, you don't have unlimited amounts of money to invest. Your decisions have to be good ones. One area where investors consistently fall down is in mistaking a fad, or a promise of one, for a trend. Advertising and marketing are designed not only to persuade consumers to buy but also to persuade investors to purchase the equities behind the products. When you see an ad for Verizon, for example, and they tout their network, the ad is telling the consumer that his or her call will get through, but the same ad is also telling the investor that Verizon is a strong, stable, growing company worth investing in.

Those dual messages are everywhere, and it is up to you to learn how to sort through them to determine what is hype and what is real. Let's look at car advertising. Everyone claims to have the best cars, the most innovative designs and technology, and the best prices, yet some companies, such as Ford and GM, are clearly not doing well, while others, such as Nissan and Toyota, clearly are. It's easy enough to say "Buy Toyota and Nissan," but nobody believes car advertising anymore, and everyone believes the conventional wisdom that car companies are not worthwhile investments despite the rise in both GM's and Toyota's share prices.

Conversely, during the late 1990s, any stock with ".com" in its title could attract a following, even though many of the companies that were raising money in the equity markets had no practical plan for earning a dime. At Winter Capital, we unloaded all our directional tech stocks after I watched Super Bowl XXXIV on January 30, 2000, when all of the advertisers were dot-coms whose only business was the ad they'd just placed, and before AOL and TimeWarner announced their unfortunate merger. My reasoning: Those companies were spending $2 million a minute of shareholder capital for no other reason than that they could. That is no reason for an investor to remain confident in a company. Their ads were meant to promote the verve and swagger of the Internet companies, but to me, swagger with nothing real behind it is a sign of weakness, and weakness is a signal to sell.

So, how do you figure out when a company is telling the truth and when it is attempting to sell its customers and investors hype? Sometimes you have to go out and kick the tires. Once upon a time, you could read the reports of Wall Street analysts and get lots of information. Those days are not over, but even those reports do not tell you as much as you need to know. Analysts used to be the terror of CEOs, because they would show up at a company, do a "sit-down" with the chief financial officer, get a good long look at the books, and then ask tough questions of the CEO. They would then share this information with their large institutional clients, who in turn would throw more business their way. Much of this came to an end after 2001, for two reasons. First, the SEC forced many brokerage firms to separate their research businesses from their brokerage arms, so that conflicts of interest would be reduced. (Brokerages used the information their analysts generated to help their investment banking arms create M&A opportunities. That practice came to an end.) Second, as large institutions became ever larger shareholders of large and medium-sized companies, they began to win seats on corporate boards.

Suddenly, they didn't need the analysts to tell them what was going on inside a company, because they were, in effect, on the inside. I hate to return to Warren Buffett all the time, but one of his great advantages is that he sits on the boards of most of the companies in which he invests, so he has an insider's perspective on changes. He can help move a company in the direction he believes will generate the best returns for shareholders. You can't.

With analyst help harder to come by, you have to do a little bit of the analyst's work for yourself. (Analysts are not gone, and the overwhelming majority of analysts at large firms are extraordinarily intelligent and extremely diligent about their work.) I mentioned before that you should become a voracious consumer of information and file away facts constantly. But you should also go out into the world and see for yourself whenever you can. You don't need to go into ten Wal-Marts and count the flow of customers to know that they serve a lot of people. Their numbers are likely to be sound, because the company is under constant scrutiny. But you might go into a Wal-Mart or two one weekend day and observe what people purchase. These kinds of "marketplace checks" are invaluable in helping you fill in information about companies. You won't learn enough from watching customers at one store, but you will add another dot to your emerging patterns, and every dot counts. Often, when you do a marketplace check, you are looking for subtleties. If it's Halloween, you want to be looking at the candy aisle. Most candy companies do the bulk of their sales around Halloween, so when you see people choosing one company's candy over another, you are looking at a clue. Some years ago, one of the major candy companies decided to install new inventory software in its warehouses the summer before Halloween. When the software didn't work as planned, the company could not get its candy into the stores. Smart investors noticed that and shorted its shares.

Don't just look at what is right in front of you for opportunity. If you see something that doesn't make sense, try to find out why. If you see an empty shelf, ask the store manager whether they have run out because supplies are tight or because the stock was bought out quickly. Either way, you have a clue that may translate into an opportunity. If the answer is that they did not receive enough stock, don't be afraid to call the company. Ask them why. Sometimes companies will let information slip because they don't know it is important. It could be that there was a temporary jam in production, which would have little impact on future prices, but maybe it was a larger problem, such as a raw materials shortage, which would have a larger impact on a company's sales. It's up to you to find out which it is.

American companies, perhaps more than their Japanese counterparts, are relentless in looking for ways to improve productivity and efficiency. So read the computer magazines to find out whose systems are being installed where, and whether there are glitches. A smooth installation means that the company may earn another couple of cents per share in improved operations and reduced costs. A holdup can mean just the opposite—and an opportunity to short the stock.

Sometimes, what looks like a fad can be the start of a trend. When Apple introduced the iPod in October 2001, nobody could tell if it would be a fad or a trend. There were already dozens of other portable music players on the market, and neither the iPod's hardware nor its software was developed by Apple, so there was some question about whether or not the company would support it if sales were not strong right from the beginning. If you were reading the news and opinion surrounding the iPod back then—a welcome relief from all the news about terrorism— there were some compelling arguments against the iPod's success.

But genuine followers of Apple noticed that the company had also begun a retail strategy, opening its first store in May 2001. A store needs a variety of goods to sell, both moderately priced aspirational goods to draw in customers and higher-priced goods to generate the profits. The iPod drew the crowds; the computers would earn the money. As it turned out, the faddish iPod became the trend; the iTunes software provided an easy mechanism for consumers of music to purchase songs at a reasonable price. With all of the conflicts regarding the copyright theft of music over the Internet, iTunes provided a sensible compromise. Those investors who could put all of the disparate elements together—the stores, the iPod, iTunes—were rewarded with a sharp jump in Apple shares.

Can you make money from a fad? Charles Ponzi did, and so did his early investors. Ponzi's original scheme was to buy international postal coupons in countries like Spain and Italy, where the exchange rate was low, and resell them in the United States, where it was higher. A coupon that sold for one cent in Spain would cost one-sixth of a cent in the United States, an exchange rate, in effect, of six to one. With that knowledge, Ponzi claimed that he could earn investors a 50 percent return in forty-five days or 100 percent in ninety days. As money began to flood in, Ponzi's scheme, which made a certain logical sense, was overwhelmed immediately, and he began paying off old investors with the proceeds brought in by new investors. Within a few months his scheme collapsed. Ponzi's offices were closed, a couple of banks failed, and he went to jail. Today, with overnight air freight, computers, and a good distribution network, his scheme would probably work a bit better, until the arbitrage of exchange rates began to narrow under the weight of the volume of transactions. Indeed, Ponzi's scheme sounds remarkably like the carry trade, and that it can be done without fleecing investors is what has kept it legal, but every now and then a money manager comes along whose ability to take in funds outraces his ability or skill in investing them, and then a story pops up in the news about some manager who has run off with his clients' funds. (This does not, of course, include those who are merely criminals, and who intend from the beginning to defraud their clients.) The clients, burned by trusting in the underlying idea, learn a bitter lesson.

Another consideration with fads is timing. Right now, we are sitting in the midst of an energy supply-and-demand imbalance. Worldwide energy demand continues to rise, and worldwide energy supply is flattening or, according to some, continuing to grow but just more expensively. Either way, it opens the door, seemingly, to opportunity in the form of alternatives. Ethanol, wind, solar, coal, nuclear, geothermal, and all sorts of variants promise to provide additional energy, if they can attract sufficient investment. This creates opportunity, but that also goes for a broad range of faddists and even outright scam artists who peddle fuel additives, devices for increasing auto fuel efficiency, or the next great alternative investment. How do you evaluate them all? You do it in the same way that you evaluate any other investment opportunity. It takes some reading, a little digging, and lots of Googling, but nearly every bit of information you need to make a sound decision on energy alternatives is already available to you and other investors. You just have to take the time to look.

CHAPTER 17

BOTTOM OF *versus* TOP OF
THE BARREL   THE BARREL

It's one of those interesting curiosities that in a forty-two-gallon barrel of oil, the last five gallons—the proverbial bottom of the barrel—are far more valuable than the first thirty-seven. How can that be? Well, when the oil is refined, the lightest components become gasoline and kerosene and jet fuel, which sell for a couple of dollars per gallon. The next heaviest component becomes heating oil, which also sells for a dollar or two a gallon. What is left at the bottom of the barrel is the heavy, tarlike residue that is turned into thousands of different organic chemicals and pharmaceutical compounds. The products of this precious goo sell for anywhere from a few dollars a gallon to thousands of dollars a pound. That paradox, that the "worst" of the lot can be worth more than the "best," also applies to investing.

Buying the bottom of the barrel is what value investing is all about. Back in the 1920s, Benjamin Graham, who taught finance at Columbia University, analyzed a host of stocks and market conditions and came up with a formula to determine what the "true value" of a stock ought to be. If an equity was priced below its true value, according to Graham, it was a "buy," but if it sold above its true value, it was a "sell." Graham's formula helped him earn millions of dollars for his clients and, later, for his disciple Warren Buffett. Graham bought stocks that were priced out of favor and then waited for some combination of market forces and management reform to change the perceptions of investors. The price of the stock would then drift upward.

What was true for value stocks also turned out to be true for "fallen angel" stocks, stocks that had previously commanded ratios well in excess of normal market returns. Whereas value stocks meet Graham's strict criteria for returns and growth, fallen angels tend to be growth stocks. Often called "story stocks" in the early days, as they depended upon a lot of narrative hype to get them going, they deliver on their growth promises for a while, at which point investors think they are going to grow forever—whether they meet such criteria or not. When they don't meet these unrealistic expectations, they become fallen angels.

As growth stocks usually do not pay dividends, while value stocks always do, some of the "value" in value stocks is the dividend. Graham considered dividends to be a form of compensation to investors for holding a stock when it is doing poorly and a total-return kicker when the price is rising. These fallen angel stocks, if they had a poor quarter or two, would come crashing to earth and would typically fall more than 40 percent in value. Worse, even after they recovered, they would typically continue to lag the broad indexes by that same 40 percent margin for several years, long after the bad news surrounding the company had burned away.

Investors, once bitten, are more than twice shy. But that may not be the right decision. In the past two years, companies that have seen their share prices stagnate have become increasingly willing to release a bit of cash in the form of dividends and share buybacks. Dividends and buybacks were supposed to lift the prices of S&P 500 shares in 2005 and 2006, but that lift has largely not materialized. Why? Well, interest rates were rising at the same time that dividends were rising, for one thing. In a rising-interest-rate environment, an investor can earn more by sitting in cash or bonds than by taking a risk by investing in stocks. Moreover, as we saw from CAPM, the higher the risk-free return goes, the greater the burden it places on shares not just to perform but to outperform in order to justify an investor's faith in them. That might be easy to do when the economy is robust and growing, but as I write this, the economy is beginning to cool. According to analysts, this cooling sets the stage for what is called a "flight to quality." Investors purchase the shares of the best companies, those with the best managements, best growth prospects, and best dividends, and then wait for interest rates to fall. It is a strategy that might make sense if you are prepared to wait, but Americans have now been waiting for years for something to happen. Each year that they continue to wait without results is another year that their investments erode in value due to inflation.

The "flight to quality" strategy makes sense if you are just coming off a very good set of returns in a risky environment and want to park your money in high-quality stocks as a form of insurance. Right now, though, the risk-free return is high, and a quality stock with a strong dividend or buyback policy gives you a similar level of return but with a lot more upside potential. A 10 percent improvement in the stock price of a company with a price/earnings ratio of 15 only means that the P/E is going to go to 16.5, which is still not expensive in today's market. But you've got the 3 percent dividend and the 10 percent gain, so now you have a 13 percent return.

Quality stocks will not move up in tandem, but rather sector by sector, depending upon the state of the economy. If the economy improves, financial shares will generally improve first. If the economy falters, look at consumer staples. Housing stocks will not do well until interest rates fall significantly, as many people now have adjustable rate mortgages that are repricing upward.

There are other ways to look into the bottom of the barrel. Often, industries and technologies fall out of favor the same way that fashion or design becomes passé, only to return later as retro but hip. That has happened in the analog electronic chip industry several times. Each time there is a new breakthrough in microprocessor technology and more and more features are loaded onto a tiny chip, someone declares analog chips dead, and the stocks tumble. A few years later, as the applications to which the new digital chips are being applied become ever more complex, a new breed of analog chips becomes necessary to handle such simple functions as turning the power supply on and off or switching between functions. Suddenly, one of the old-line analog chip makers comes back into prominence, and its stock shoots upward. The same kind of cycle holds with electronic instrument makers and the manufacturers of equipment to make each succeeding generation of chips. Each new machine is millions of dollars more expensive than its predecessors, but each is more crucial than the last, due to the improvements in productivity that it offers and the cost reductions that it creates. Fewer of the new machines may be sold, but their cost more than overcomes the drop in volume. The same thing holds for the shares of these companies. They can rise very rapidly on very little volume, because they are being followed by only a handful of investors, until suddenly, they are no longer bottom of the barrel but rather 10 A.M. investments.

Indeed, you do not need to look for fallen angels when looking at the bottom of the barrel. The vast majority of stocks on all exchanges show little movement from day to day. All you need to do is to go through a couple of sectors in a systematic way and look for a sector that might move in the next six months or so. Begin your research the same way you would any research, gathering and collating. You will begin to see patterns emerge, and then you can invest in the companies in the group with the best market share, the strongest balance sheets, and the best record of bringing new products to market. Most of the time, you will have picked winners, but even when you don't, remember that ten is fourteen ahead and four back.

What is true for bottom of the barrel stocks is also true for bonds. Junk bonds, as they are called, can pay huge returns. They also have a high risk of default, except when they don't. Between 2004 and 2006, the default rate on junk bonds dropped to historic lows, and as of this writing, defaults are still extremely rare. On the other hand, junk bonds now have yields close to that of Treasury notes, which means that they are not worth buying, since you are taking on uncompensated risk. But if the default risk is so low, why not? I am not advocating that you put your entire portfolio into junk bonds—there is too great a possibility that you will get burned—but investors who have a higher tolerance for risk might want to squeeze a few extra fractions of a cent out of the bonds in their portfolio by looking for value in high-yield credit, especially if the bond environment remains tame. If the default rate rises, bail quickly. Don't wait for your own bond to be the next victim.

Not only are there junk bonds, but there are also junk nations. It is easy for a nation's sovereign credit rating to be downgraded by the bond agencies if monetary or fiscal policies fall out of line with accepted norms, and when that happens, a nation is forced to pay higher interest rates. Brazil has a booming stock market and has paid off its debts to the IMF, yet it still has government bonds that pay a high interest left over from its last bout of financial instability. In order to be bailed out, the Brazilian government had to issue bonds that it guaranteed it would not call. These are difficult to find, however, because they provide a substantial income for some Brazilian investors, and Brazil's balance of payments is still not strong enough to provide a negotiated settlement. So for now, at least, when such bonds become available, they are a high interest reward with diminishing risk. As you go downward in the credit quality of nations, look for such imbalances. They are everywhere, and when investors find them, they represent new opportunities.

CHAPTER 18

KNOW-WHO *versus* KNOW-HOW

The phrase *red tape* derives from the era immediately following the American Civil War, when veterans who wanted to gain benefits from the government had to present their cases in portfolios bound in a specific kind of red ribbon. The producer of the ribbon earned a guaranteed living at the taxpayers' expense.

Around the world, innumerable arrangements such as the red tape example enrich one or two individuals or families and ensure their fortunes. Likewise, there is a vast army of "fixers" in the developing world, people "to see" if you want to get something done. It isn't called bribery any more, because U.S. law prohibits American companies from paying bribes. It is called "the cost of doing business." It could be the large number of tax stamps and permits you have to get in order to start a business or a license only issued periodically and then only to the highest bidder.

According to Hernando de Soto, author of *The Mystery of Capital,* many developing nations are poor either because they lack clear titles for property or because they have created too many roadblocks to the transfer of titles. To start a business in Egypt, for example, it takes more than three years and several hundred different permits covering everything from the square footage of the store to each employee's salary, and they all have to be filled out in the proper sequence. That provides a good income for the people who have a government concession to sell tax stamps, but it does little for the Egyptian economy. In such societies, people with "know-who," the right family ties and the right connections, stifle the initiative of the people with know-how, the entrepreneurs and businessmen who have the talent to grow the economy.

The question, then, is, in whom do you invest? In a society where change is neither apparent nor on the horizon, the people with know-who will always trump those with know-how. Indeed, when Russia privatized industries after the dissolution of the Soviet Union, a handful of oligarchs who knew the system snapped up many of the shares of newly privatized companies at the expense of ordinary citizens. Now, as the Russian government gradually forces these newly minted billionaires to cash out, good investment opportunities have come to the fore.

In other societies, such as China, know-who and know-how increasingly coexist, to the benefit of both. China is a rare example—Vietnam is another—of a nation in which state control remains strong but business is also booming. While ideologues run the government, there is an open agreement: if businessmen stay away from politics and confine themselves to making money, the businessmen will be facilitated with bank loans from government-controlled banks, permits to purchase real estate, and, sometimes, the privilege of eminent domain. That's know-who at its best, and when it is coupled to successful enterprises, it can propel rapid growth for an economy.

For the average investor, though, know-who is a leap down the rabbit hole. It is all but impossible to figure out who has real power. You might read a story in one of the financial magazines about a suddenly rich businessman, but you will have no knowledge of his contacts in government, and most likely, neither will the reporter. On the other hand, you can assemble information based upon what you see. If you notice an excess concentration of development in a single city, it is an almost sure bet that the local administrators have extra power with the central government. Such was the case with Shanghai in China for more than a decade. The government in Beijing winked and nodded as a small group of administrators surrounding Shanghai's mayor flouted most of China's rules and built a huge and prosperous city. When corruption got too out of hand, a lower-level administrator would be arrested from time to time, a warning to the mayor of Shanghai not to go too far. As long as such arrangements persist, growth continues and an area remains safe for investment.

The danger with know-who is that it can disappear in an instant. In a large nation such as China, with a stable Communist Party, change will occur slowly. But since the inner workings of the party are closed to out-siders, the impact of a given change in leadership—who the new "who" are, so to speak—is unpredictable until after change begins to take place. That leaves you further along the dial, less able to make a winning invest-ment. Worse, in a smaller nation like Vietnam, or even in a democratic nation like Thailand, cadre shifts can and do take place literally overnight, and policy changes can be swift. While we as Americans like to believe that because we "won" the Cold War, the world now sings a capitalist tune, that just isn't so. Many nations are parting with their oligarchic past with reluctance, whether the group in power comes from the left or the right. Nobody gives up power willingly. In Yugoslavia in the 1970s, when Marshal Tito was still alive, he made certain that each ethnic group re-ceived its rightful share of bounty—an auto plant in Serbia, a dairy plant in Montenegro, a steel mill in Croatia, and so forth—concessions Tito was able to extract by playing the Russians against the West during the Cold War, until he died in 1980. That system went on, but when the Cold War ended in 1989, there was no one left to distribute the bounty and no bounty left to distribute. Provincial leaders began to beggar one another in a race for the remaining crumbs. As Yugoslavia was already a patch-work of ethnic groups and religions, leaders began to exploit these differ-ences with an increasingly virulent set of verbal attacks on each other, which almost inevitably led to widespread violence as the ethnic tensions that had been papered over for two generations exploded into bloodshed. While the now independent nations that were once Yugoslavia struggle to rebuild, it will take another generation to get back to where they once were. That is a consequence of know-who gone awry.

The problem with betting on know-how instead of know-who is that while it rarely results in bloodshed, it is often just as difficult to ascertain who is ahead and who is behind. When a new technology emerges, it is rare that only one company has it, and when there is a widespread tech-nology challenge, it is all but certain that dozens of companies will spring to life, all fueled by venture capital, all looking to wrest a place in the sun and in investors' hearts. Investors seeking to understand know-how have witnessed overinvestment and destruction cycles in computers, chips, digital phones, MP3 players, and dozens of other technologies. But this process is not new. Back at the beginning of the twentieth century, there were over three hundred automobile companies in the United States alone, each asserting a technological claim to leadership. Within fifty years there were five. Within eighty years America was down to its "Big Three," which is now really two, as one is owned by a private equity firm. In biology, nearly five hundred firms were started in the 1980s and 1990s; they burned through roughly a trillion dollars in venture capital, yet today there are only a handful of publicly traded biotech firms.

How, then, do you choose? This is one of those cases where you really do have to follow the experts. In an immature technology, it is almost impossible to sort out potential winners from losers. You could purchase a whole basket of stocks and hope that there is one big winner that will be larger than all the rest of the losers, but that's a risky business. You could purchase that basket in the form of a mutual fund devoted to a single new technology and hope that the manager is much better versed in the technology than you are. He might balance his portfolio to yield a better return, as he will discard the bad choices earlier than you might. Or you can avoid the choice altogether and pick an industrial sector such as housing, where knowledge is widely disseminated. The returns won't be as great, but neither will the risks.

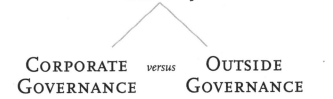

CHAPTER 19

CORPORATE *versus* OUTSIDE GOVERNANCE

Who controls a company? Its management, its shareholders, or the original founders of the company? Who owns what often determines the decisions a company makes and in whose interest it makes them?

After every major downturn in the stock markets, there are calls for reforms to protect the investing public. Investors who have lost a substantial amount of money accuse companies of acting in bad faith and sue, or the Securities and Exchange Commission or, increasingly, state attorneys general or the European Community will step in and demand greater transparency in the operation of companies on behalf of shareholders. "One share, one vote" shareholder democracy is supposedly the antidote to company boards placing their own interests above their shareholders'. As with everything, though, this is an investing area that is not black-and-white but gray.

For sure, there are closely held companies that fall into the habit of self-dealing, awarding contracts to close relatives or putting favorites on the board. But then again, there are widely held companies that are supposedly paragons of shareholder democracy with the same bad habits. Tyco International was a paragon of corporate openness when Dennis Kozlowski became CEO in 1992, as it remained through his two trials and ultimate conviction for grossly overcharging the company for his personal expenses. Conversely, the Washington Post Company has always been closely held, with all of the voting "A shares" held by the Graham family. This ownership has not stopped investors from placing large, and largely successful, bets on the company's growth prospects. While in general well-run, widely held companies perform better in the long run, you

are attempting to become a better investor, so you are looking for companies run to be profitable *while you own the shares,* even if the CEO is maximizing short-term gains and forsaking the future.

I know that this runs counter to everything that you have read in financial magazines and newspapers. But remember that journalists, like academics, don't run companies. They are pundits on the sidelines. If you
want to do better as an investor, part of your job is to think like a CEO. If
there is a short-term gain to be had, you have to learn how to take that
gain and then move on. The average chief executive now lasts longer than
he or she did five years ago, according to management consultancy Chal-
lenger, Gray, and Christmas, but the rapid management changes that
continue to happen in the United States are caused as much by the ac-
tivism of hedge fund managers and private equity firms as by the Eliot
Spitzers of the world. Investors with large amounts of capital at stake, especially capital that belongs not to them but to their own investors, are
judged by results, so a poor-performing hedge fund or private equity firm
will see its capital dwindle rapidly. As a result, these funds place unremit-
ting pressure on CEOs to make decisions that maximize shareholder
value in the present, even if those decisions are not so good for the company in the future. Since Wall Street bets on the future and discounts the
present, companies often lose long-term value by maximizing short-term
returns.

A decade or more ago, a takeover battle meant that shares might rise to
a substantial premium. Now, with private equity a major force, the trend
is all downward. The equity firms want a low price at takeover so that
when it "fixes" the company and brings it public again in a few years, the
differential between the purchase price and the selling price is as large as
possible. As an ordinary shareholder, that's not in your interest. So what
do you do? In between the time that a private equity firm first evinces interest in a firm and the time when that firm is taken over or the original
management is overthrown or changed, the company will often attempt
to find a quick fix for one or two of its problems. General Motors is in the
process of doing that. Kirk Kerkorian bought up a large enough stake of
the company to force GM to take on some of his team as board members,

and for more than a year, he attempted to force GM into making major changes. The CEO, Rick Wagoner, has resisted, but he has begun to speed up GM's efforts to get its pension liabilities under control while continuing to work on the problem of GM's stagnating sales. The result has not been a takeover but a 40 percent or so rise in GM's stock since Kerkorian entered the fray, which was enough so that in November 2006 he sold his shares. If you had ignored what you had read in the papers and magazines about GM's failures, you might have participated in that run-up. With its share price up, Wagoner's resistance to forced outside change has stiffened, and Kerkorian has walked away from GM, albeit with a nice profit.

What is happening at GM is happening at scores of other companies, and it will continue to happen to scores more over the coming years. Investors used to a continually rising stock market, especially large investors, are increasingly willing to pool their money into large private equity companies and to use that money to force change to elevate share prices. When they are thwarted, as they are at companies such as *The New York Times,* which concentrates decision-making and share-voting power in the shares owned by the Sulzberger family, they demand shareholder equality and democracy. Such demands can be painted as hypocritical, since private equity investors—for that matter, all investors—knew the share structure before they invested. Indeed, it is perhaps doubly hypocritical for long-term investors in the *Times,* since they profited handsomely when the company was doing well under exactly the same share arrangement. Back then, no one questioned the business acumen of the Sulzberger family. But again, Wall Street doesn't care about yesterday. It cares a little about today and much more about tomorrow. As should you. Many of the shareholder activists who say they are looking for better governance are really looking for a better deal. As Austrian economist Joseph Schumpeter wrote, capitalism is about creative destruction, with the emphasis on destruction. If it is a choice between the destruction of a nice proud institution and the destruction of your shareholder value, side with the breakup against the possibility of losing money. I am a great believer in better corporate governance as a rule, because I know that over the long term, it produces better results. But my job in this book is to help you search out opportunity in the here and now and not in some dreamy future.

The question of who controls the company is even more important when you invest globally. American investors rarely ponder the question "Who's in charge here?" They assume that the rules governing companies are pretty much the same for all countries, similar to those in the United States. While it may be that accounting rules are becoming more similar and that shareholders can read a European or Asian balance sheet and have a better idea of what it means, governance rules vary widely from nation to nation.

Germany has the third-largest economy in the world and is far and away the most prosperous nation in Europe. But should you invest there? Few shares are held directly by individuals, other than the founding families of the company, and most of the control of the company is in the hands of boards composed of managers, union members, representatives of larger social groups, bankers, and government officials. Where are the directors who represent the shareholders? There aren't any, because the shareholdings are often indirect. Some investors might purchase shares directly on German exchanges, but more likely, if you are a German citizen, you are going to own shares through funds controlled by your union's pension plan or by your insurance company. They will have seats on the board, and whatever problems exist will be settled inside the boardroom, free from pesky independent shareholders. Many of these companies are well run and competitive in world markets, but often, when it comes to decision making, shareholder rights take a backseat to social needs. If unemployment is high, the unions and the government members of a board argue that it is bad social policy to add to unemployment by firing workers. If it is a choice between increasing the dividend to the shareholders or increasing social benefits to the workers, guess who gets the short end of the stick?

It's not just in Germany that government intervention acts as a brake on corporate governance and decision making. For years, the Dutch electronics maker Philips was a world-class innovator, Europe's equivalent of Sony, but always far less profitable as the company's board gave away its excess profits to its workers, discouraging shareholders and, ultimately, new investment. Japan's companies for decades guaranteed lifetime employment to workers, because when the policy was put in place, nobody ever dreamed that there would be so many aging workers or that the booming Japanese economy would ever slow. But both happened, and government interference in corporate governance has prevented Japanese companies from making the dynamic changes needed to remain competitive. That has helped to keep Japan, until quite recently, mired in recession and deflation for more than ten years. As an investor, you don't care whether the interference in a company's ability to grow comes from government, embedded shareholders, or poor management. You want any company in which you invest to have a fair chance. Otherwise, why bother?

CHAPTER 20

WIRED *versus* WIRELESS

If I asked you to choose between putting your money into a wireless company or an old-line telephone company with a vast investment in conventional copper wiring, which would you choose? At the end of the 1990s and the turn of the millennium, that choice looked easy, as investors worldwide rushed into wireless as the latest and greatest technology. Alas, they were badly burned, as wireless companies built vast amounts of capacity in towers and repeaters for growth that would take years to materialize. In the United States in particular, consumers have been very slow to take up all of the many value-added services now offered over wireless telephones—photographic and movie capability, downloadable music, concierge services, and on and on. Why are Americans so resistant compared to consumers elsewhere?

The answer is mobility. Wireless phones allow consumers unlimited mobility. For millions of Europeans, Asians, and Latin Americans, that mobility is a newfound freedom, so each new service that is offered only adds to that sense of mobility. In the United States, our mobility comes from our cars. When we want to see someone or share an experience, we don't need picture phones. We might use our wireless phones to call friends, but then we jump in our cars and drive across town and see them. Americans are also planners and schedulers. If we want to do something, it is cross-checked against our personal schedules of work, family, and play. When an event meshes with the schedule, it is added, and again, we jump in our cars to get to the event. In the United States it is not uncommon for people to drive for hours to go to a concert or a sporting event or to attend a family reunion. For longer distances, people are very quick to hop on a plane and fly across our large country.

In less-affluent nations, the phone has become the substitute for being there. (Indeed, long ago, AT&T, when it first introduced domestic dial-up long-distance service, used the advertising tagline "The next best thing to being there" to convince consumers that the service was worth spending money on. Now there is no "next best thing to being there." Being there is easy.) In several African nations, for example, cell phones are used for personal banking, and money can be wired to any of thousands of pickup points in nations with few ATM machines. The fees paid at the pickup point are no higher than ATM fees—indeed, they are often cheaper. In Asia, wireless phones are used to order merchandise, to turn on appliances at home before you arrive, to turn on the lights, and to perform hundreds of other services for which there are other methods in the United States. As a result, the U.S. cellular and wireless markets are light-years behind those out in the rest of the world, and while the cellular companies are beginning to prosper, it is largely by raising their fees, not through value-added services. When the average American gets his or her first car at sixteen and the average person in the rest of the world is in middle age before he or she owns one, the gap in how people use technology becomes almost unbridgeable. Even rising fuel prices will probably not make much of a difference, as American habits are extraordinarily ingrained. (Readers who use Blackberries may disagree, but you are in a very small—though growing—minority. Introduced in the late 1990s, Blackberry to date has secured barely 7 million users, almost entirely for business. Compare that to 207 million U.S. cell phone subscribers.)

Are wireless companies a good investment? As you go down the development scale, the lower a country's mean income, down to about three thousand dollars a year in purchasing-power parity, the more investing in a wireless company makes increasing sense. In countries like Brazil, Argentina, Mexico, and Venezuela in Latin America, and in Asian nations such as Indonesia, Thailand, and, of course, China, wireless usage is exploding, and wireless companies are at the top of the local stock markets. This boom has several years to run, and as even more value-added services are offered to a rising middle class, wireless companies will continue to ride high, much in the way computer stocks did in the United States between the mid-1970s and 2000. Wireless is the productivity tool of the rest of the world, and those who invest in productivity tend to do well.

Meanwhile, the traditional wired companies have undergone years of mergers and of pruning away deadwood, and they have emerged even stronger than ever. They have learned to sell their capacity to Internet providers and cellular companies that need to move large amounts of data across long distances and that are locked in near-mortal combat with cable companies to provide services to the home. Once rivals, wireless companies have become the saviors of the wired companies, as so much service has now moved to wireless that it is cheaper for wireless companies to buy capacity from the conventional telephone companies than to build new wireless capacity. Moreover, as new services such as VoIP—Voice over Internet Protocol—become ubiquitous, these services also need to purchase capacity from those who have it, namely the old-line wired telephone companies. Companies like Skype, the Estonian firm that is currently the world leader in VoIP, will use more and more traditional phone company capacity, making them profitable for several more years at least.

Will that come to an end? It's difficult to say. A couple of years ago, experts were predicting the outright demise of the conventional telephone companies, yet here they still are, in good financial health. The problem with technology is that few people can accurately predict its path. Companies that appear destined for the scrap heap can find new vitality and new uses for the technology they already own simply by adding new services or by modifying their technology. In a world that values the new, it is easy to dismiss the tried and true, but often, if the foundation is sound, technology can be continually retooled and rebuilt. The old telephone companies have done a better-than-average job of reinventing themselves and supplying their services to new customers, which makes you wonder whether other old-line industries, such as the chemical industry or mining, can learn to do the same. At the end of the day, it is not better technology that gives one company a lead over another. It is the willingness of management to find north and then head toward it.

CHAPTER 21

COMMON *versus* NONSENSE SENSE

When you are inside your own home, you are, to a certain extent, the master of your castle. The moment you walk out the door, you depend upon the rule of law to keep you safe in an otherwise hostile world. Earlier I wrote that you should generally align your interests with those who are attempting to force profits out of companies in the short term, because, like them, you are looking for opportunity and should then be prepared to move on. But you also have to align yourself at least partially with those who are interested in maintaining the rule of law, especially when it comes to protecting your investments. Every year, unwary investors are bilked out of hundreds of millions of dollars in illegal schemes that are transparently unsound, by promises of magnified riches and opportunity. Every year, the SEC, the U.S. Postal Service, and state attorneys general convict and punish dozens of perpetrators of investment frauds, and every year, new frauds arise, each one more sophisticated and more subtle than those from the year before.

These frauds are not perpetrated only by hucksters. They are increasingly created by governments hungry for foreign direct investment. A nation can appear to place itself on the path of reform, as Russia has, and still not have foreign investors' best interests at heart. Such nations, if you want to invest in them, are best invested in indirectly, through mutual funds, indexes, and ETFs. In a nation where the rules are unclear and where the ground shifts dauntingly often, you don't want to build your investment house directly on shaky ground.

This caution does not apply solely to stocks or bonds. More and more people in developed nations are purchasing real estate in very distant locales, whether it is Americans in Mexico, Costa Rica, and the Dominican Republic or Britons in Romania and Hungary. On paper, the land ownership laws appear airtight as to who can own what, but in many nations, titles and deeds are still a free-floating subject, with more attention paid to the lawyer who drafted the contract and his influence than to the law underlying the contract itself. The opportunities can appear grand. A home on Hungary's beautiful Lake Balaton, an estate in Baja California. It sounds appealing. But when you purchase from a distance, you don't know the full extent of your protections, and you have no idea who is going to enforce them. If you don't understand all the risks, you should tread with extreme caution.

The same is true if someone approaches you to invest in a business outside your own area of expertise or neighborhood. If it is inside the United States, you can make a trip to look at the business, or you can hire someone with a reliable reputation. Even then, you have to invest carefully and ensure that you are contractually protected. Once you step outside the United States, you should not proceed without the help of the best and most politically influential law firm in the nation or nations in which you plan to operate. A law firm is no guarantee against seizure, but at least you will have some recourse. And, of course, there is insurance, from the Overseas Private Investment Corporation. OPIC is an independent agency of the U.S. government that sells insurance and provides investment information to those contemplating investing in businesses abroad. OPIC is very good at what it does, and it is an excellent source of information about investment prospects in different nations, especially emerging economies. Other government agencies, such as the Department of Commerce, can also help you with potential investments abroad.

Obviously, you should avoid any business or investment opportunity that has even the whiff of fraud about it. If someone promises you immense tax-free returns, they are likely making an illegal promise, because the net cast by the U.S. Internal Revenue Service is now almost universal. Practically the only way a U.S. citizen can avoid taxes is not to have an investment in his or her own name—but when you do that, you also have few protections if something goes wrong.

There is a still larger issue involving the rule of law. Nations undergoing reforms meant to strengthen banking, finance, investment, and property are more attractive to outside capital than those that are not. Many investors talk about the worldwide swell of liquidity sloshing around the investment community. It is true that there are trillions of dollars available for investment, but much of it remains in cash not only because of investor nervousness about uncertainty but also because there are simply not enough good investments. By "good investment" I do not only mean one that will provide a better-than-average return, I also mean investments that won't dwindle down to nothing without any chance for investors to recoup. When you look at the world as a global investor, you see a patchwork of possibilities, some good, like India, where markets are well managed and the rule of law is strong, and others, like China, where despite the huge opportunities, it is still more advisable to invest indirectly, if only because the rule of law is uncertain. It is the difference between Brazil, whose economy has slowed considerably but whose rule of law gets stronger every day, and Argentina, which now has a rapidly growing economy but government and laws that are still not stable. It is the difference between Chile, where the rule of law is well embedded, and Venezuela, where the rule of power routinely supersedes the rule of law. It is the difference between Russia, where the rule of power resides in the persons of the oligarchs, and the Czech Republic, which has made huge strides since emerging from Soviet domination. Nations that have improved the administration of the rule of law have been rewarded with rapid growth and diminishing risk. Nations that have been slower to institute legal protections have also seen rapid growth, but at higher risk levels and with no guarantee that investors will not someday look to pull out. You, as an investor who wants a good return without all the headaches of risk, should look for nations where you can feel safe investing and leave the riskier regions to others.

PART V

THE CLOSING BELL
Choosing a Money Manager

The binaries covered in this book address many of the choices that an investor must use to make good decisions, but the binary technique is perhaps as important as the binaries themselves. Smart decision makers learn to reduce decisions to simple yeas or nays—not simply with regard to investments but for all of their decisions. For example, when I began working for Citigroup, early on in my career I had to decide how I could be most effective. I made up a list of binary behavioral decisions that define leaders and managers, which I believed would determine the difference between whether I grew on the job—and thus the institution with me—or not. Here they are:

What Managers Do	vs.	What Leaders Do
Position one's expertise	vs.	Afford broader understanding
Power	vs.	Empowerment
Information "need to know"	vs.	Information "needs to know"
Control	vs.	Revenue
Permission	vs.	Results
Centralize decisions	vs.	Facilitate decisions
Authorize access	vs.	Encourage access
Process and procedure	vs.	People
Self-define issues	vs.	Listen to issues
Solve own problems	vs.	Solve others' problems
Give instruction	vs.	Give thanks
Keep in the dark	vs.	Keep enlightened

In business, you are surrounded by people in both columns, so you have to ask yourself, where does your enterprise intend to make the most money over time? Which approach will produce the highest return? If you are searching for a money manager, which approach do you think will give you a better return over time? Left-column managers tend to wind up as middle managers but in general do not attract or retain talent. The choices on the right, those I attribute to leaders, are the decisions that produce the best payoff and the most satisfied customers, if for no other reason than that they build confidence in your customer base and help bring you a closer understanding of customers' needs. All too often, in the money management business, clients buy into a "style," which is not only an investment methodology but also a set of managers' behaviors. Many managers and professional investors who are successful in the short run follow the precepts on the left. Those who build enduring businesses, successful both in the returns they earn and in the way they treat customers, adhere to the precepts on the right. Even the best money managers have poor years, and when they do, if they are not treating their customers properly, they are going to lose not only income but also principal through withdrawals. There are many managers in the marketplace, and a disaffected client can always take his or her capital someplace else. A money manager who practices the behaviors in the right-hand column and makes sound investments will build a following that stays over time. Know your manager if you can—learn, observe and study his or her long-term track record.

If you take a close look at that list, you will see that it is also a set of behaviors worth following simply because they will help to keep you focused on what is important. Even if you are not that much of a team player and have strong personal ambitions, you have to know that those who facilitate good decisions are rewarded, so why hoard information that impedes sound decision making? Likewise, if you are in some kind of gatekeeper role in your company, you know that you have the power to control access. But opening the gates as wide as you possibly can lets others in, and it is their participation that can help your company grow.

This set of binaries is useful in lots of other ways. It can help you decide with whom you want to do business, and not just in investing.
How does your bank or your telephone company treat you? Are they always giving you reasons why they can't help you and controlling the
flow of information, or are they constantly looking for new ways to
make your life easier and to avoid disputes rather than wasting your
time while you attempt to settle them? Now take that to another level:
which of those companies do you think will be a better investment? If
you take a look at growing companies that are consistently successful
in their own marketplaces, they are generally firms that make life simpler, better, and more reasonable for their customers. I'm not the first
person to understand this: Peter Drucker said decades ago that the
mission and purpose of any business is to satisfy its customers. That
doesn't mean that the customer is always right, but it does mean that
listening and learning is the best way to please a customer. Companies
that can listen and learn almost invariably figure out new ways to increase their profits. That is, in fact, what I do for a living. Yes, I travel
around the world and speak to clients and bankers about the things I
do and what I see, and I attempt to put events in perspective for clients
who want some idea of how to proceed. But as I noted way back in the
Introduction, I am a listener. Many of my best ideas originate with
clients. They are far more attuned to what is going on in the world,
from a real-life perspective, than I am, because if they are wrong, their
businesses suffer. Take a family textile business in New England, for example. Over the years, they have regular family meetings, and years
ago, they decided to move most of the business to South Carolina to
take advantage of lower labor costs. For years their abandoned mills
were a local eyesore, but there was nothing they could do about it, and
besides, the real estate taxes were low. Sometime in the 1990s, the
family had to decide whether to close their mills in the Carolinas and
reopen in China. Part of the family disagreed, and spun off the Carolina
mills as a new company. The other part took the abandoned real estate
in New England and opened a partnership with Chinese mill owners.
Who do you think has done better over the past decade? Not only has
the part of the family that moved its business to China prospered in the

textile industry, but the old mills were renovated and sold as expensive riverside residential lofts and weekend vacation space. The portion of the family that made its stand in the Carolinas? Out of business. My employer's clients are confronted with decisions like this every day. I don't try to give them advice but rather try to open their eyes to the realities of the world. It's their money, but by taking the position that I am here to help *them* solve *their* problems, not mine, I keep their trust and, ultimately, help them to become more successful.

I hope that I have helped you to steer clear of the clutter of contradictory information and chatter that confronts today's investors, and that I have helped you to understand that the decision-making process is often as important as the decision itself. If I have done that, you will become a smarter and better investor.

CHAPTER 22

CONVENTIONAL *versus* ANOMALIES WISDOM

In his book *The Wisdom of Crowds,* James Surowiecki argued that if you believe in the "invisible hand" of the marketplace, then you have to believe that most people, most of the time, will make the right decisions. Extended to investing, this argument suggests that investors make the right decisions most of the time.

If that is so, how is it that so many of them do so badly so much of the time? Remember that the vast majority of investors waited for more than a decade before they made the switch from bonds to equities, even though interest rates had already come down past the point at which the relationship clearly favored equities. Why did so many investors lose out on the early opportunities? Because they had convinced themselves that what they knew was right and that what they were seeing every day was wrong.

Another way of looking at this problem is to examine information efficiency. Economists have long argued that the markets are essentially perfect, reflecting all available information and all investor sentiment accurately. Yet we know that investors clearly get it wrong a lot of the time and that stocks move up and down for reasons that often make little sense. There are many cases of stocks that lay moribund for years, despite the value that was locked up in them. That's why investors like Mike Milken and Carl Icahn were able to earn fortunes in the 1980s and why private equity firms and hedge funds are earning fortunes today. They saw the value and invested when nobody else wanted to. Then they promoted the value until other investors understood, allowing them to sell, often at huge profits.

There is lots of information inefficiency left in the markets despite the wealth of information that comes at us 24/7 from news outlets all over the world. The question is why. I can suggest several ideas why this might be the case.

First, the huge number of new entrants in the markets distorts the information flow. Not only do we now have American, European, and Japanese views of the markets, we now also have the views of millions of other investors around the world. Just as we see the world through our telescope, they see it through their microscope. While as investors, we used to outnumber them substantially, their numbers are growing every day, which means that their views increasingly prevail. Behavioral finance is a big subject these days, as academics attempt to understand why investors make the decisions they do. But if we don't understand why, for example, an Asian investor sees the world differently from an American investor, we will never be able to make truly sound decisions.

Right now, the Chinese government owns nearly $1 trillion worth of western bonds, mainly U.S. Treasury notes. Other Asian nations own nearly another $1 trillion. In classical economics, that money should return to the United States because Asians will be fearful of it losing its value. They should be using their money to purchase U.S. goods or industries or real estate, as they did the last time a large imbalance built up. But they are doing no such thing, and U.S. policymakers are attempting to force the issue, in the form of one treasury secretary after another going to China and pleading with the Chinese to allow their currency to float upward. What we all fail to understand is why the Chinese and other Asians are content to sit on their money, even while the U.S. dollar drifts downward. Yet the answers are right in front of us.

We know that Asia's populations are aging. We know that Asia still needs enormous amounts of capital for development, and we know that most Asian nations have a capital deficit that forces them to import the capital they require in order to meet their developmental needs. If you know these three things only, you can begin to understand why Asian nations are content to sit on their dollars and to continue to lower their own prices in order to retain access to American markets. If you also consider that many Asian nations have suffered more than one bout of financial disaster in the last decade, you can begin to see why Asians hold on to their money. It's their behavioral finance that matters, not ours. Until American investors take this into account, they will not make good decisions regarding Asia.

A second reason for information gaps is that there are not enough people to integrate all the information. This factor is not well understood, yet it pervades nearly every discipline of modern life, from microbiology and the study of DNA to finance. We are drowning in data points. There are not enough people with a sufficient body of knowledge to digest them all and to make sense of them. That is why we are so often blindsided by events, even when they are of critical importance. The National Security Agency, the FBI, and the CIA had nearly all of the information they needed to capture the 9/11 terrorists weeks, even months, before the attacks. Even if there had been no bureaucratic infighting, even if all of the information had been shared, and even if the possibility of an attack from al-Qaeda had not been downplayed, it is doubtful that we would have been able to sort through all of the information and put it together in exactly the right way to prevent a tragedy. Perhaps we might have stopped one of the planes, perhaps two, but a plot of that scale would have overwhelmed our defenses, despite our best efforts, simply because there were too many data points.

A third reason that we cannot make sense of what we see as easily as we used to is that events now happen with an increasing simultaneity. We often don't know which event to react to. Was it the July 4 liftoff of the space shuttle or the July 4 missile launches by North Korea? Was it the G-8 summit in Saint Petersburg, which was going to focus on Iran's nuclear weapons, or the simultaneous attacks by Hezbollah on Israel that helped to touch off the destruction of Lebanon? Those who profit from events have always attempted to control the flow of information to their advantage, but in our age of global television and the Internet, that has become easier, as we, the viewing and reading public, are left confused.

Finally, the number of data points is on the rise because the number of actors has increased. When there were half a dozen stock and bond markets that we cared about, we knew that events in one market had a certain degree of correlation to events in another market. If Brazil or Argentina had a financial blowup, investors in Hong Kong knew that their markets were going to be dragged down, because investors in the West simply lumped all emerging markets together. That process is called "contagion," and once upon a time, it was probably a good way to handle investments that you didn't understand very well. If it didn't make sense, or if it looked bad, it was quicker and safer to throw the baby out with the bathwater. But nowadays, that's a recipe for creating anomalies and opportunities.

Out of these factors, three types of anomalies arise: short-term anomalies are based on misperceptions of information, while medium- and long-term anomalies are based on structural shifts that are not yet widely understood. A good example of a short-term anomaly took place in 2004. Investors were so wild about China and its enormous GDP growth that they failed to notice that Chinese companies were suffering from production bottlenecks. A few Mexican companies noticed and pitched themselves as backup manufacturing capacity for the U.S. market. As a result, Mexican equities as a whole rose 27 percent in 2004 before reaching a plateau in 2005, as Chinese companies ironed out their problems. If you had been alert, you would have noticed the rise in the Mexican stock market, understood its causes, and cashed in.

An example of a long-term anomaly is the problem of natural gas. The conventional wisdom says that the world is running out of energy, but current natural gas reserves are equal to about a hundred years of oil production. The problem is, gas is difficult to transport and is not readily available in the markets that need it. As a result, gas prices have soared, even as natural gas sits in the ground for lack of a transport mechanism. The smart investor knows that this situation will not remain unremedied and so begins to invest in companies that make pipe, in pipeline companies, and in shipping companies building gas transport ships, and so on. The payoff might not come for a few years, but that investor will have invested just as the problems were being solved, so the value of the investments begins to rise.

Are anomalies another way of looking at the visible yet incomprehensible? No. Visible yet incomprehensible problems are generally larger and last longer. Anomalies, as the name implies, are simply distortions in the flow of information that, once recognized, quickly come to fruition as investments and then disappear. Yet I believe that the number and variety of anomalies will continue to increase in the coming years, at least until investors come to grips with the much larger and far more variegated shape of today's markets. Anomalies may not be giant waterfalls, but they are waterfalls nonetheless, and when you find one, it's a sure bet that you can place your bucket underneath and increase the value of your portfolio.

CHAPTER 23

ONE FINAL WORD

I started this book with the admonition that successful investing takes hard work, alertness, and a willingness to open your mind and learn. I'll close it by giving you a couple of hints about where I believe the next waterfalls might be. If you have been reading diligently, you will have already come up with a good number of investing perspectives that ought to convince you that if you do your homework, it is possible to become a successful investor. You should have acquired the tools with which to make sound decisions and to eliminate indecision so that you can act when you see an opportunity, wherever it exists.

To begin with, look at emerging markets. In the past decade, more than two billion people have emerged into the lower ranks of the middle class, and there are at least another billion waiting to follow, principally scattered throughout Asia, Latin America, and central Europe. There is also an emerging middle class in southern Africa that is slowly spreading northward. As these people begin to spend money, they are going to take care of the basics first—better and more food, better clothing, and better housing. Since opportunity increases as people move to cities, these new consumers are going to need urban infrastructure—clean water, a reliable power grid, sanitation, and decent transportation. While individuals will be climbing up the ladder, their nations will still find it difficult to attract funds for infrastructure development, so money for health care, education, and retirement will probably have to come out of household budgets. That probably won't leave much left over for luxury goods, but in each emerging nation an entrepreneurial class is developing that is supplying these needs, and those entrepreneurs will become the nucleus of tomorrow's high-net-worth individuals who *do* consume luxury goods. Every one of those needs is an investment opportunity, and as the rule of law takes hold in nation after nation, investment opportunity will grow.

As the middle class grows in these nations, energy needs grow as well. In a poor nation, energy consumption might be as low as 1,000 kilowatt-hours per person per year. In the United States, it is more than 13,000 kilowatt-hours per person per year, and in households with computers and lots of home entertainment appliances, it is rapidly passing 20,000 kilowatt-hours per person per year. That increase in energy, plus the growing number of vehicles on the road, means that there is a growing need for more energy to be extracted from the earth. That drives the demand for increased investments in energy infrastructure, both in traditional fuels such as oil, gas, and coal and in alternatives such as gasohol, wind, solar, and hydropower. Those investments cost money, and in a world of $100 barrels of oil, they provide a good return on everything from tankers and pipelines to refineries and storage facilities. More good investments, both in emerging markets and in the developed world.

At the same time that the world wants more energy, it also wants a cleaner planet. There is now only a small market for clean energy and for the technologies to provide it, but those technologies will attract an ever larger share of investments down the road. Markets are already developing in carbon trading, and carbon sequestration—the process of pumping carbon dioxide into underground storage facilities—will likely become a standard technology within a decade.

Above all, in a world of harder-working individuals, surcease will always be valued the most. Travel, leisure, the ability to get away to a vacation home or a resort, the chance to do something different, someplace else, even for only a while, will engender possibly the single most important group of industries to emerge in the twenty-first century. Alongside health care, which will be ever more pressed to provide a better quality of life for billions of people, travel and leisure will dominate a future world.

And what about uncertainty and the fears with which we live? These will not go away, I'm afraid, anytime soon. Wooing young dispossessed people from terrorism and crime depends on the growth of jobs and the availability of quality education, and both are in short supply around the world. It is a simple but regrettable fact that for the moment, productivity growth is outpacing job growth around the world. That creates legions of dispossessed youths, and in nations where those youths constitute a majority or a large minority of the population, they will also constitute a threat to the security of the world. At the very least, they will be a source of endless migration, itself a large, and largely intractable, problem. At worst, these dispossessed youth will be the source from which succeeding generations of terrorists could be recruited. Without education, these young people will not be able to step into an increasingly complex world, so education is bound to become a major source of investment in the future—and a major source of earnings.

The last place you might imagine opportunity to be, but where it will likely be huge, is right here in the United States. American investors will wise up in several ways that are familiar to investors around the world: They will learn to diversify their investments away from dependence on the strength of the dollar, they will learn to buy insurance against every investment, and they will become savers against the chance that yet another bubble will come along and wreck an investment, whether it is in equities, bonds, or real estate. The first, currency diversification, only makes sense. The dollar will likely recover, but if you plan to do business abroad or to travel, or if you are going to become a global equity or commodity investor, at least some of your portfolio needs to be in currencies that rise when the dollar falls. That means learning about which currencies are up and which are down and acting accordingly. It might turn out that it is advantageous to purchase Turkish equities as much because the Turkish lira is appreciating as because the stocks are outperforming.

As for buying insurance, I have said this many times throughout this book, but I will say it again. When volatility is low and insurance is cheap, nobody buys it, and when volatility in the market explodes, no one can afford it. You insure your house, your car, and your life. Some go to Las Vegas and buy insurance at the blackjack table. Learn to buy insurance, in the form of options, on your equities. And finally, become a lot more dedicated in your savings. As I noted at the outset of this work, before you can invest, you have to have a nest egg, and before you have one of those, you have to accumulate some surplus. That is done in only four ways:

spend less than you earn (the old-fashioned, Dickensian way); earn at a faster rate than you spend (the aggressively capitalist path); learn how to winnow out what is unimportant (the Zen path); or make certain you are going to inherit. All too many Europeans a couple of generations ago, and Asians only a decade or so ago, and Latin Americans many times, have had to learn these lessons. Now it is our turn.

The other great opportunity for Americans is going to be in real estate. I know that sounds odd right now, but a mortgage credit crunch means there is going to be a lot of very cheap real-estate paper floating around very soon, and properties are going to be available for fractions on the dollar. It is a harsh fact of capitalism that one investor's profit is often another person's pain, and there will be lots of pain before the current mortgage crisis ends. But there also will be tons of bargains. Many people looking at the lofty prices that apartments and houses go for in New York City forget that only forty years ago, you couldn't give New York City real estate away. There is a community in the northern New York suburbs called Tuxedo Park, built in 1886 by the millionaire Pierre Lorillard IV as a resort for socialites of the day. By the Great Depression it had been all but abandoned, until a new group of people began buying up the great old houses during the 1970s and fixing them up. Today, they are again worth a lot of money. So real estate will almost certainly come back, with lots of new owners.

I am told that it is never good to end a book on a pessimistic note, and ending it with millions of potential uneducated terrorists and a real estate crisis doesn't sound too good. But it is meant to be a challenge. Every problem does indeed represent an opportunity, and many of them represent grand investment opportunities. It is up to you to keep your eyes open and to invest wisely. I am certain that most of these problems will create their own solutions and that capital will flow toward all of them. How do I know this? Twenty years ago, if you had come to Silicon Valley's venture capital community with an alternative energy idea, you would have been laughed out of the room. Now, every month, there is a venture capital conference on the subject. Capital is always attracted to the best opportunity, as are the smartest people. Those who have great wealth know that they can lose it in an instant if unrest boils over. The days when small cliques were willing to exploit their own people is now almost over, and we are entering an era of increased social responsibility among high-net-worth individuals. And not just for charity's sake, but because they understand that by providing better goods and services to ever greater numbers of people, they are only protecting their own existing fortunes. Comprehension of the world's problems is what makes me optimistic, and it is why you ought to be optimistic as well. A world of opportunity is about to unfold. All you need to do is be there.

Acknowledgments

For years I've had the good fortune to meet with and listen to a large number of individuals who have made themselves successful in business, the arts, and other walks of life. I've also encountered some people who offered advice that, if implemented, would have had devastating consequences. Having lived on three continents in good and bad times, having witnessed remarkable leaders and destructive demagogues, I became increasingly aware that the forces of success and those of failure are really quite distinct.

For a long time, I primarily tried to understand and observe the forces of success, but over time I've learned that how failure develops is also important, for therein lies great opportunity. As a student of the arts, I learned initially from great artists whose own awareness, when shared, offers us new dimensions of understanding. None have been more generous or more insightful to my learning within the arts than Robert Frank and June Leaf. As artists, they see the world with ever-fresh eyes, which is a trait that they have in common with successful investors. Within the business of business, I've learned from some of the most successful investors in the world. They have so many distinct ways of seeing the world that their individual aspects combine like facets on a diamond to create a single, shining jewel that is valuable precisely because all the facets work in harmony to reveal the diamond's inner fire.

Several years ago, some friends and colleagues suggested that I string these diamonds together into a book. I was initially reluctant, but I was encouraged by Steve Kindel and Mark Reiter; they worked with me to distill these diamonds into a series of dichotomies, which helped me, as I wrote, to string them together within a context that others might understand. My hope is that by sharing these ideas, I might help investors feel more confident in taking control of their destinies. The world ahead will undoubtedly offer a series of challenges, and I hope that our work here will enable some leaders and decision makers to make wiser choices. I want to thank those whose wisdom and generosity are great gifts, but I also want to acknowledge the contributions of those whose poor judgment taught me the paths to avoid. This is yet another dichotomy, and the understanding and resolution of dichotomies is so much the determinant of success in all areas of existence, not simply investing.

INDEX

ABOUT THE AUTHOR

CLARK WINTER is director of portfolio strategy and managing director of Goldman Sachs & Co. Prior to joining the firm, Winter served as the chief global investment strategist for Citigroup Global Wealth Management, Citi Private Bank, and Smith Barney. He founded Winter Capital International, an independent advisory firm that was acquired by Citigroup, and has also worked at JPMorgan. He regularly appears on CNBC and is frequently quoted in *Financial Times*, *The Wall Street Journal*, and on Bloomberg. Winter is a member of the International Council of the Belfer Center for Science and International Affairs at the John F. Kennedy School of Government at Harvard University.

About the Type

This book was set in Scala, a typeface designed by Martin Majoor in 1991. It was originally designed for a music company in the Netherlands and then was published by the international type house FSI FontShop. Its distinctive extended serifs add to the articulation of the letterforms to make it a very readable typeface.